GOD—OUR CONTEMPORARY

By J. H. JOWETT, D.D.

God—
Our Contemporary

By
J. H. JOWETT, M. A., D.D.

NEW YORK   CHICAGO
Fleming H. Revell Company
LONDON AND EDINBURGH

New York: 158 Fifth Avenue
Chicago: 17 North Wabash Ave.
London: 21 Paternoster Square
Edinburgh: 75 Princes Street

Foreword

ALL the sermons in the present volume have been born in my mind and heart during the last two years and they were preached in the course of my regular ministry at Westminster Congregational Church. I think it will be found that they centre in the controlling conviction that it is only in the fuller reception of God's grace, and in the more matured understanding of His will, that we can find a sufficiency of resource to meet all the pressing perplexities of the soul, and all the wider problems which attach to the reconstruction of human society. God is the dwelling-place of all generations, and our generation will find in Him the light for all requisite vision, and the strength for all our appointed tasks.

God, in Christ Jesus, is our great Contemporary. " The same yesterday, today, and forever."

J. H. J.

London.

Contents

I

WHERE OUR GREATEST BATTLES ARE FOUGHT

"Men ought always to pray and not to faint."
—LUKE xviii. 1.

THAT word was spoken when the Master's noon-tide was already past. The shadows were lengthening upon the way, and some of the Lord's sayings breathed the air of coming night. The road was heavy with deepening gloom, and now and again in the windings one caught the glimpse of a cross. The disciples were startled into confusion. The happenings ran athwart all their expectations. The things which the Master was speaking about were a brutal defiance of their fondest hopes. They had been looking for a golden harvest, and now the snow was falling. They had been eagerly anticipating the faily coloured dignities of dominion, and their eyes were now turned upon the black trappings of defeat. They had been stepping forward to a kingdom, and to the shared sovereignties of a throne, and now a scaffold begins to loom at the end of the road. And so their minds were all at sixes and sevens. They were torn with uncertainties. They were distracted with doubt.

9

Fear, too, came into their hearts with chilling menace. And some of them were tempted to retreat. Others became weary and heavy in their goings. Others again began to faint.

And in our Scriptural passage we have one of the Lord's specifics which is to be used against the assault of circumstances, and the threat of impending doom. What is this specific which makes one master of the changing way? " Men ought always to pray and not to faint." The guiding word may mean that men are always to pray and never to faint in prayer. Or it may mean that men ought always to pray and they would never faint even when antagonisms rear themselves like awful mountain ranges between them and their goal. It is probable that both interpretations are equally true and that both are included in the Master's mind and purpose. For the cardinal matter is this; the heavy emphasis which Jesus Christ puts upon the ministry of prayer as a predominant means of grace. " Men ought *always* to pray." The fellowship is to run through all the changing seasons of life, through spring and summer, and autumn and winter. " Always to pray!" In the springtime of life, when the blossoms are forming, in the winter when the snow is falling and the trees are bare! When we are sauntering through the green pastures or toiling across the wilderness! In the playfield or in the battlefield! In the winsome dawn which sheds its light upon the marriage altar,

or in the empty darkness which gathers about the
tomb. " Men ought *always* to pray." Such is the
fervent pressure of the Master's word. And what
He urged others to do He was always doing Himself. He prayed always. He prayed in the brilliant sunshine when the multitude would have taken
Him by force and made Him a king. He prayed
in the night in which He was betrayed,—when all
others had fled. He prayed in the open fields when
He was feeding a famished crowd. He prayed by
the grave of Lazarus. He prayed in the midst of
the pestilence that walketh in darkness; He prayed
in the midst of the destruction which wasteth at
noon-day. Most surely He exemplified the counsel
which He gave to His disciples when He said that
" Men ought always to pray."

Now let us consider one or two primary matters
concerning this mighty business of prayer. And
let us say first of all that the ministry of prayer is
not entirely one with the exercise of petition.
Prayer and petition are not synonyms, two names
for the same thing. If the realm of prayer finds
its symbol in some noble estate, then petition is like
one field on the landscape. And there are seasons
of prayer when we need not be in that particular
field at all. Our spirit may be wandering in
other parts of the wide domain. I am not dis-
paraging the mighty prerogative of petition. But
I am saying that it is only a part of our spiritual
inheritance.

> Thou art coming to a King,
> Large petitions with thee bring.

Yes, I know it, and there are seasons when I would come to the King, burdened with intercessions, and I would spread the world of my necessities before the favour of His grace. I am coming to a King, but I am coming to more than a King. I am coming to a Father, and Fatherhood is larger than Kinghood, just as home is larger than a throne. A king may have gifts at his disposal, he may have honours and benefits and offices to confer upon his subjects; but fatherhood moves in a circle of intimacies and shared secrets, even in the matchless commerce of truth and grace and love. When prayer turns into this marvellous realm it is not so much a suppliant, laden with petition, as a wondering child walking in the revealing companionship of the Father in heaven. Prayer is not always like Lazarus, clothed in rags, and bowing in suppliancy at the rich man's gate; it is sometimes like Lazarus in the Father's bosom, dwelling in the secret place of the most High, and walking and talking in the shadow of the Almighty.

I may be pardoned for dwelling upon this distinction, as I think we are not always conscious of the range of the inheritance of the saints in light, and we only occupy a corner in our Father's house. I was once present at a prayer meeting, and one led us in prayer who was very evidently a disciplined traveller in the realms of grace. He left the field of petition, and he went wanderingly and wonderingly along among the unsearchable riches of Christ as though he were straying among the amazing glories of matchless woods. And the leader of the meeting bore with the traveller for some time and then broke out impatiently, " Brother, ask God for something! Ask God for something!" But the brother did not seem to have anything to ask for just then; it was quite enough to be walking with his Father in the boundless realms of grace. "Ask God for something!" No, prayer is not always petition, sometimes it is just communion. It is the exquisite ministry of friendship. It is the delicate passage of intimacies; it is the fellowship of the Holy Ghost.

Now let me state a second primary matter concerning this mighty business of prayer. If it is not always in the form of petition neither need it be always in the form of words. I want to try to say something which is very real to me, but which almost refuses the clumsy ministry of expression. There is a very vital part of prayer which can do without the vehicle of words. We can escape from the burden of the limitation of words. Who has not felt the bondage of speech, the cumbersomeness of words when he has sought to pray? And who has not experienced the peril of living words becoming dead forms? The lithe, nervous, blood-filled words have stiffened into corpses, and all our prayer has been dead. How often it happens that we do not possess our words; we are not their owners. They are not our children, coursing with hot blood which has been gathered at the springs of our own life. How often our words have no vital communion with us, and when we are not their owners we become their slaves. So there are times in prayer when I long to escape from the ministries of words, and to have wordless fellowship in the Presence of God.

This is what I mean. First of all, we quietly and reverently put ourselves into the Presence of God, we collect our scattered consciousness in the sense that God is near, and we come before His Presence. How is the Presence revealed? Who can say? Are there any means or methods which men and women have practised in the realization of the Presence of the unseen Friend? Yes there are, but I suppose we must say that there are almost as many ways as there are people who have practised them. Some call in the aid of a devout imagination, and in the secret place they realize a face, even the face which was unveiled to us in the Nazarene. To others the sacred Presence assumes no form, because there is no image which their consecrated imagination can frame which seems worthy of their unutterable devotion. Horace Bushnell led his spirit into a certain bright luminousness in which the Presence of the Lord was veiled, and he communed with Him in the light. That is also the way of a very dear friend of mine who is greatly learned in the things of grace. His spirit withdraws in the Presence of a shining splendour, and there he holds his fellowship. Others have nothing of this kind at all. They just recall themselves into God's Presence and without any image of form or any sense of light they know and feel that God is near. But these differences do not really matter, and it is well for everyone just to take the way which gives them the most intimate assurance of the Presence of God. Here is one soul about whom I have recently been reading.

"Well, as I was saying, when we got to the woods, Mercy stayed in a little grass path by the edge, and opened a very dull-looking book, and I went into the wood alone. At first it was awfully thick and tangled, and all alive with little winged and feathered things that darted off quickly or rose with a whirr. I love that, don't you—all the stirring of bunnies and dickie birds in a wood? Then I got to a little clearing and sat down on a fallen tree in the sunshine. The sky was blue, blue, the kind of blue that goes on for ever, and the little shadow of leaves all lacy on the grass. It was just Beauty, and nothing else—almost better than music! Then, as I looked at the intense blue of the sky, I changed, from knowing Beauty, to knowing Love. Of course, I can't begin to tell you, but I felt I was in the presence of God. He was around me like light, like showers of light, and like love. I wanted to kneel, but I could not move. I could not think at all for a minute—' a minute,'—I don't know, it might have been a second or an hour, for all I know. Then my mind said, ' This is Life. Now I know."

But I think it is not necessary for us to emphasize anyone's particular way as being the way for others. Never mind another's way, seek your own. Recall your spirit into the silence. You may not necessarily be in solitude; it may even be in the midst of a crowded train. Withdraw into the secret depths of your own spirit. Quietly say to yourself that the Eternal God is near who revealed Himself in Jesus Christ our Lord. You may be perfectly sure that you will become more expert in this sense of discernment as you continue in its practice. You will realize that you are in the Presence of God. And now, as you realize it, introduce in that Presence anything which concerns you and in which you have a vital interest. Let your imagination rest on that thing, and quietly bring it to the sacred silence where you are closeted with God. See it clearly, and then, with great deliberateness, introduce it almost visibly into the sacred Presence. That is to say you are now intelligently and imaginatively bringing some interest into the heavenly places, and you are setting it in the light of God. That is again to say, you are thinking of something while your mind is suffused with the sense of God. You are bringing the two into fellowship, you are setting them face to face. You need not utter a word, you can escape from the crude bondage of your own ignorance, and from the narrow limitations of speech. You offer no verbal petition, but you set your human concern in the mighty and pervasive influence of the Spirit of God. There must be no irreverent haste. There must be no frivolous tramping of the holy courts. It must all be done with patient deliberateness, steadily holding the interest, whatever it be, in the holy light of God. And no words are needful.

Suppose the vital interest be your own child. Well, then, set yourself in the sacred silence, with a sense that you are near your Lord, and then, with alert imagination, bring your child into the holy place. See him there, hold him there. And what are you doing? You are establishing vital currencies between him and the divine Presence, and you can do it without the ministry of words. Of course, you may speak if you will, but I think your words will be few. For in setting him there in the silence you are praying, and you are presenting him to the grace and wisdom of God, and your dedicated homage is providing channels for the river of the water of life.

Or it may be some personal habit which constitutes your vital concern. Or it may be some particular piece of business. It may be some loss which you have suffered, or some great gain which you have made. It may be a bride. It may be a widow. It may be an orphan. It may be a people, a race or a tribe. It may be one of ten thousand things. I am urging you to practice this means of grace, in thus introducing our interests to the sacred Presence of the Almighty. See them there, and hold them there, and whether it be with words or without words, whether in verbal devotion or in attitude and act, you are carrying out something of the Master's counsel when He said, " Men ought always "—in everything and everywhere— " to pray and not to faint."

Well now, it is in the field of prayer that life's critical battles are lost or won. We must conquer all our circumstances there. We must first of all bring them there. We must survey them there. We must master them there. In prayer we bring our spiritual enemies in the Presence of God and we fight them there. Have you tried that? Or have you been satisfied to meet and fight your foes in the open spaces of the world? If I am like Bunyan's pilgrim, and encounter Apollyon on the exposed road, and begin my warfare there I shall be sadly beaten, and he will leave me bruised and broken by the way. My resource is to immediately get him into the field of prayer and engage him there. The struggle was going against Bunyan's pilgrim until he changed the manner of his fighting.

" Apollyon as fast made at him, throwing darts as thick as hail; by the which, notwithstanding all that Christian could do to avoid it, Apollyon wounded him in his head, his hand, and foot. This made Christian give a little back; Apollyon, therefore, followed his work again, and Christian again took courage, and resisted as manfully as he could. This sore combat lasted for above half a day, even till Christian was almost quite spent; for you must know that Christian, by reason of his wounds, must needs grow weaker and weaker.

" Then Apollyon, espying his opportunity, began to gather up close to Christian, and, wrestling with him, gave him a dreadful fall; and with that Christian's sword flew out of his hand. Then said Apollyon, ' I am sure of thee now.' And with that he had almost pressed him to death, so that Christian began to despair of life. But, as God would have it, while Apollyon was fetching his last blow, whereby to make a full end of this good man, Christian nimbly reached out his hand for his sword, and caught it, saying, ' rejoice not against me, O mine enemy; when I fall I shall arise,' and with that gave him a deadly thrust, which made him give back, as one that has received his mortal wound. Christian, perceiving that, made at him again, saying, ' Nay, in all these things we are more than conquerors through Him that loved us.' "

I am, therefore, trying to say in the spiritual realm what Lord Fisher once said in the realm of material warfare. He said, " Compel your enemy to fight you on your own drill ground." Yes, indeed, and when we fight the world, and the flesh and the devil on the drill ground of prayer, we have a certain victory. Let us bring our evil thoughts on to the field of prayer. Let us drag our mean judgments on to the field of prayer. Let us drive our ignoble purpose on to the same field, and our insane prejudices, and our malicious practices, and our tyrannical passions. Let us fight them on our own drill ground and slay them there. Men ought always to bring their evil antagonisms and besetments into the Presence of God. Force them into God's holy place and there fight and slay. Men ought always to pray, and they will not faint in the heaviest day.

And on the same field of prayer we must bring our troubles, for we get on to the top of them in the holy place. It very frequently happens that many of our troubles lose their fictitious stature when we bring them into the Presence of the eternal God. They shrink when we set them in a large place. It is almost amusing how little things appear big when they are set in confined and narrow spaces. Put them in a bigger field and they lose their alarming size. And there is many an anxiety that looks gigantic until we set it in the holy field of prayer in the Presence of the Lord. Aye, and there are other things which seem enormous and overwhelming until we set them in infinite relations. Sometimes a grave seems so big that it appears to fill the world. There is nothing in the world but the grave. When we see it on the fields of communion and in the glory of the light of the risen Lord, captivity is led captive, as death itself is buried in the eternal life of God. It is not our father's purpose that we should see our dead in cemeteries, but rather in the heavenly fields of the infinite love; and it is there that death loses its cold and cruel servitude. It is when we compel death to go with us on to the fields of divine communion that the grave is seen to be only a vestibule of the life indeed. "O death, where is thy sting?" "O grave, where is thy victory?"

And even when some of our troubles remain, as indeed they will, it is on the fields of prayer that we get above them, and assume and assert our sovereignty in the power of the risen Lord. We have a very familiar phrase which, I think, is very suggestive. We say, "Under the circumstances!" But why should we be under them? Why should we not be regnant above them? Why slaves and not masters? Why under and not above? It is on the field of prayer that we get our circumstances beneath our feet. "Thou shalt tread upon the lion and the adder, the young lion and the dragon shalt thou trample under feet." "Ye shall have power to tread on serpents." "I keep under my body and bring it into subjection." That is the purposed sovereignty which is ours in Christ. And we daily assume the sovereignty and we ride our enemies on the wonder-working fields of prayer. Said Lord Fisher, "Fight your enemy on your own drill ground." Very well, then, lead your troubles on to those holy fields, and get above them in the emancipating grace of the Lord.

But prayer has larger relationships than any of these. I can not only bring my spiritual enemies on to the battle field of prayer and slay them there. And I can not only bring my troubles into the expansive realm of prayer and ride them as the Creator rides the storm. I can bring the burdens and necessities of humanity into the sacred Presence, and in my own life I can become a point of vital contact between God and the human race. For I am not a unit of mankind, isolated and independent, a being of separated interests, self-centered and self-contained. I am just a fraction, a single member, a limb, a mere fragment of humanity, and I am indissolubly connected with it. The solidarity of the human race is inclusive of me, and I am a vital and indivisible part. The moral and spiritual blood of the race runs through me, and through me it circulates throughout humanity. When, therefore, I commune with God in prayer I become a point of contact, an inlet through which the divine life flows into the veins and arteries of humanity. That is no idle figure of speech. Every man is an inlet through which clean or unclean energies pour into the general life-pool of the human race. We cannot help it. My points of contact determine the character of my contributions, and if my supreme contact is with God in the communion of prayer, I become an open channel through which the blessed influences flow into human fellowship for its eternal good. And so the prayer-ground is the common ground of racial enrichment. The hands that make contact with the battery direct the electrical dynamic to every fibre and tissue of the body. And hands that are uplifted in prayer are conductors of the divine dynamic to the general brotherhood of humanity. And therefore our Master counsels us to retire into the secret place. Create a sensitive quietness about your spirit. Realize the sacred Presence. And then slowly and deliberately, in the holy place, present your helpmeets and your antagonisms, your privileges and your necessities, your banes and your pains, your laughter and your tears. And in your life the ancient miracle of grace shall again be wrought, for the Son of Righteousness shall arise upon you with healing in His wings.

II

BRINGING HEAVEN TO EARTH

"Thy will be done on earth as it is in heaven."
—Matthew vi. 10.

I SUPPOSE that to the majority of people these familiar words suggest a funeral rather than a wedding. They recall experiences to which we were compelled to submit but in which we found no delight. They awaken memories of gathering clouds, and gloomy days, and blocked roads, and failing strength, and open graves. "Thy will be done!" They remind us of afflictions in the presence of which we were numb and dumb. And so we have a sort of negative and passive attitude toward the words. We have a feeling toward them as to some visitor we have to "put up with," rather than to a welcome friend whose coming fills the house with life and happy movement. They suggest the cyprus and the yew tree, things sullen and gloomy, rather than the coronal attributes of the cedar and the palm.

And so it is that the graces and virtues which are most frequently associated with these words are of the dull and passive order. The grace of resignation is the plant which is most prolific in this bitter

soil. Even many of the hymns which sing about
the will of God are in the minor tone, and they
dwell upon the gloomier aspects of Providence
which call for the grace of resignation. I am not
unmindful of the fields of sadness which often
stretch around our homes like marshy fens. Our
circumstances gather about us in stormy cloud and
tempest, and the rains fall, and the floods cover our
lot in dreary desolation. And we may reverently
recall one black night in the days of the Son of
Man when in Gethsemane the rains descended, and
the floods came, and the winds blew, and the afflicted heart of the Saviour submitted itself in
strong resignation, crying, " Nevertheless, not My
will but Thine be done."

And yet if resignation be our only attitude to the
will of God our life will be sorely wanting in delightful strength and beauty. A cyprus here and
there is all very well, but not a woodland of them!
A yew tree here and there is all very well, but not a
whole forest of them! In one of his letters Robert
Louis Stevenson has a paragraph which represents
an imaginary conversation with his gardener about
the black winter green known as Resignation :—

" John, do you see that bed of Resignation ? " " It's
doing bravely, sir." " John, I will not have it in my
garden; it flatters not the eye, and it is no comfort; root
it out." " Sir, I ha'e seen o' them that rose as high as
nettles; gran' plants." " What then? Were they as tall
as Alps, if still unsavoury and bleak, what matters it?
Out with it, then; and in its place put a bush of Flower-

ing Piety—but see it be the flowering sort—the other species is no ornament to any gentleman's back garden."

But then how are we going to get more of the flowering piety into our gardens? I think this is the answer. We shall get it by cultivating a more active and positive attitude toward the will of God. The will of God is not always something burdensome which we have to bear; it is something glorious which we have to do. And therefore we are not to stand before it as mourners only, humbly making our submission, but as keen and eager knights gladly receiving our commissions. The will of God is not always associated with deprivation; it is more commonly associated with a trust. It is not something withheld, it is something given. There is an active savour about it. There is a ringing challenge in it. It is a call to chivalry and crusade. And therefore the symbol of our relation to the will of God is not that of the bowed head, but that of the lit lamp and the girt loin, as of happy servants delighted with their tasks. It is in this positive relationship to the will of God that the will becomes our song, the song of ardent knights upon the road, riding abroad to express the will of their King in all the common intercourse and relationships of men. "Thy will be done on earth!" That is not merely the poignant cry of mourners surrendering their treasures; it is the cry of a jubilant host, with a King in their midst, consecrating the strength of their arms to the cause of His

Kingdom. The will of God is here not something
to be endured, but something to be done.

How, then, are we to take our share in this commission? How are we to do the will of God on
earth as it is done in heaven? *First of all, by finding out what life is like in heaven.* " As it is done
in heaven!" If our privileged commission is to
make earth more like heaven it must surely be our
first enquiry to find out what heaven is like. Well,
what is heaven like? I will very frankly confess
to you that I am in no wise helped to answer our
question by the so-called spiritualistic revelations of
these latter days. These strange séances with the
lights out, and a trumpet on the table, and the
rowdy singing, they bring me no authoritative
word or vision. The character of the heavenly life
that is revealed is so unsatisfying—the glare of it,
the garishness of it, its furnishings as of a cheap
and tawdry theatre, the utter weakness and insipidity of its utterance—they tell me nothing that I
want to know. Its leaders assure me that their
revelations are chasing away uncertainties, that
they are transforming lean hypotheses into firm
experiences, that they are proving the reality of the
life beyond, that they are making immortality
sure. . . . I am waiting for a revelation of something which deserves to be immortal. I am reverently listening for some word which is both spirit
and life. I am listening for something worthy of
kinship with the word of the Apostle Paul; nay,

worthy of the risen Lord; and what is offered to
me is like cheap jewelry in contrast with precious
stones and fine gold Eternal life is to me not
merely endless length of line; it is quality of line;
it is height, and depth, and breadth; "This is life
eternal, to know Thee and Jesus Christ whom
Thou hast sent."

I therefore turn away from the so-called modern
revelations if I wish to know what life is like in
heaven. What is life like as it is lived in the immediate presence and fellowship of God? What
are the habits of the heavenly community? What
is the manner of their affections? What is the
nature of their discernments? What are their
standards of values? What are their ways of looking at things? What are their quests, and their
labours, and their delights? What are their relationships one to another? Is there any answer to
these questions? My brethren, if I wish to learn
what life is like in heaven, I turn to Him who came
from heaven. He made certain tremendous claims,
and the very greatness of them arrests my soul and
fills me with receptive awe. Let us listen to Him:
" No man hath ascended into heaven but He that
came down from heaven." . . . " He that cometh
from above is above all; what He hath seen and
heard, of that He beareth witness." . . . " The
bread of God is He which cometh down out of
heaven and giveth life unto the world." . . . " I
am come down from heaven to do the will of Him

that sent Me." . . . What is that last most wonderful word? It seems to come very near to the way of my quest. I am eagerly enquiring how God's will is done in heaven, and here is One who claims that He comes down from heaven to do the will of Him that sent Him. He brings heaven with Him. His speech is full of it. He talks about "Your Father in heaven," He talks about "the treasures in heaven," and about "the Kingdom of Heaven," and He uses simile after simile, and parable after parable, to tell us what it is like. "The Kingdom of Heaven is like unto . . . is like unto . . . is like unto . . ." The familiar words run like some lovely and inspiring refrain. . . . If I would know what heaven is like I must listen to His word.

But the revelation in Christ Jesus is more than a revelation in words. The Word became flesh, and it was not only something we can hear, it was something we can see. He not only startled men's ears, as with a music which had never before been heard in their grey, unlovely streets, He startled men's eyes as with a light which had never before fallen on sea or land. He not only talked about the heavenly life, He lived it. His life on earth was just a transcript of the life in heaven. As we reverently gaze upon Him we can watch the process of the incarnation. The heavenly is imaged forth in the earthly, and it is taking form in human life and story. Every movement of Jesus spells a word of the heavenly literature. Every feature in Jesus is a lineament of the invisible life. Every gesture tells a story. Every one of His earthly relationships unfolds the nature of the heavenly communion. His habits unveil their habits, His quests reveal their quests. The Eternal breaks through every moment, and the light is tempered to our mortal gaze. The revelation never ceases. It begins in Nazareth and it continues to Calvary, and beyond Calvary to Olivet. You can never catch our Lord in some moment when the divine afflatus has been withdrawn, when the inspiration ends, and when His life drops down to dull and unsuggestive commonplace. Everything in Jesus is a ministry of revelation. He *is* revelation; " I am the Truth." His earthly life reveals the landscape of the heavenly fields. If, therefore, I would know what heaven is like I must listen to the word of Jesus, and with eager, reverent eyes I must follow the Word made flesh.

But let me give this counsel about the quest. When we set about studying the words of Jesus do not let us become entangled in the letter. It is possible to be imprisoned in the words and so to miss the hidden treasure. We are in search of the spirit of the Kingdom of Heaven, we want to know its attitudes, its royal moods, its splendid manners, its principles, its life. We must not, therefore, be deterred and interred in the literalism of the letter. We must seek the hidden treasure in the earthen vessel. We must seek the heavenly wine in the earthly wine-skins. We must seek the beating heart of a simile, the secret vitality of a parable, the holy fire which burns on the innermost altar of the word. We are in search of heavenly principles, principles which we can apply to the humdrum life of earth and so transform it into heaven.

Go, then, in search of the principles of the heavenly life. And whenever you find a heavenly principle, something which controls and orders the life of heaven, write it down in your own words, and regard it as one of the controlling guides of humdrum life. Do the same with the Master's life. What a brief little record it is! I turn away my eyes to my study shelves and I see the life of Lincoln in five large volumes. I then turn to the biography of Jesus, and in the Bible which I am using it covers 107 pages, and in those 107 pages the story is told four times over? How marvellously brief it is, and yet how marvellously pregnant! Go over it with the utmost slowness. You are in search of something more precious than gold, yea, than much fine gold. If our Saviour moves, if He turns His face toward anybody, if He looks at a little child, or at someone who is near the Kingdom of Heaven, follow the movement, and watch Him, and challenge your judgment as to its significance. Is the movement a revelation? Is it an earthly segment suggesting a heavenly circle, and can you venture to reverently complete the circle? Thus must we go in search of the heavenly principles, and again when we have found one let us express it in our own words, and write it down as one of the fundamental controls of human life.

And when you have got your heavenly principles, when you have analysed them, and have arranged them in some order, will you have many of them? I think not. Will your notebook be overflowing with entries? I think not. You will probably have just a little handful, perhaps not more than a dozen of them, perhaps only half-a-dozen; but they will be something you can handle, for not only are they the principles of heaven, they are the laws of heaven for our life on earth, they are the fundamental things in the ministry of transformation, and they are to make earth and heaven one. If, therefore, you would know what life in heaven is like, study Him who came from heaven, even the Son of Man Who is in heaven.

Well, now, having found out what life is like in heaven, we must now find out what life is like on earth. What are the facts about things on this planet of ours in which we pitch our moving tents for three-score years and ten? If we are to bring the principles of the heavenly life to mould and fashion our life upon earth we must know what we are about. Is our life on earth in any way like the life in heaven which is revealed in Jesus Christ, or is it very unlike it? We must go in search of the facts. What are the facts? And there you face

the difficulty which only an unwearying perseverance can conquer. For, strangely enough, it is far
more easy to discover the facts about the life in
heaven than to discover the facts about the life on
earth. Heaven yearns to reveal itself, to make
itself known, to share its secrets, and it has done
these things in Jesus Christ; but earth seeks to hide
its facts, to obscure them, to skilfully camouflage
them, until it is almost impossible to discover the
simplicity of truth in all this elaborate parapher-
nalia of falsehood and disguise.

How intensely difficult it is to see a thing just as
it is, in all the clear, vivid, untampered outlines of
sheer veracity! Our newspapers do not really help
us in the quest. Their vision is perverted in many
ways—it is perverted by political partisanship, by
the spirit of class, by the narrowing mood of sect,
by the proud domination of wealth, by the desire to
please more than to inform. How hard it is to find
the facts through the daily press! I take two
morning papers, and I have chosen them on the
ground of their being as absolutely unlike each
other as can be well conceived. I look out upon
the world through their two lenses in the fond
hope that one may regulate the other, and that in
their mutual correction I may arrive at something
like the truth. But through what a riot of confusion one has to fight his way if he is to find the
fact of things in their simple and transparent
order! For instance, the facts about the miners

and the owners of the mines! The facts about
Prohibition in the United States! The facts about
the drinking customs of our people! Where are
our working people assembling in vast multitudes
to demonstrate their determination to have more
drink? Where are the masses of people who are
assembling to demand a brighter London, and who
are going to secure it by extending the drinking
facilities for an hour or two longer at night?
What are the facts about things? The facts about
the starving populations of Russia! The facts
about India, about the inner currents of its thought
and feeling, the secret aspirations of its countless
multitudes, the sleepless activities of Islam! What
a hunt it is, this hunting for facts! And yet, if the
heavenly principles are to be brought to earth, to
govern and regulate her life, if the crooked is to be
made straight and the rough places plain, we must
know where the dangerous crookedness is to be
found on the road, and where the road is so rough
that it breaks the feet of pilgrims and lames them
for their honest and necessary journey.

I can well imagine that if the Church of Christ—
the whole Church of Christ, were united in life and
purpose, if she were really what we sometimes sing
she is—a mighty army, not shuffling along any and
every road in loose and bedraggled array, but
marching under one plan of campaign and moving
in invincible strength—I can imagine she would
have her own Intelligence Department, her own

secret service, her own exploring eyes and ears, peering everywhere, listening everywhere, knowing the most hidden facts of the nation's life, and proclaiming them from ten thousand pulpits in every part of the land. But while we wait for the united Church of Christ we must not go to sleep. Young people must strenuously and untiringly seek to get at the facts. How is it with old mother-earth? Is she full of the glory of God? Or is she full of shameful things, crooked things, wasteful things, wicked things? Is her life really vital, or is it superficial, artificial, a poor withered, wrinkled thing hidden in powders and cosmetics? What are the facts? Knowing what life is like in heaven find out what life is like on earth. Get at the facts.

And now for a last thing. Having a firm grip of divine principles—" as it is in heaven," and with a clear knowledge of earthly facts—" as it is done on earth," then with fearless application bring your principles close to your facts, and make your facts bow to your principles, reshaping them by the heavenly standards so that the crooked becomes straight and the rough places plain. Bring the heavenly close to the earthly, and change every earthly thing into heavenly currency, stamping it with the divine image and superscription. " Thy will be done on earth as it is done in heaven! " That is gloriously positive work. It is challenging work. It is exhilirating work. It is work which is worthy of the knights of God. It is to bring

heaven and earth together until the two become
one. It is to bring the heavenly to the earthly, to
bring divine principles into the region of economics, into the realm of business, it is to bring them
into the thicket of politics, to the simplification of
society and to the reconstruction of international
relationships.

"It can't be done!" What is that? "It can't
be done!" What can't be done? "You cannot
mix the heavenly and the earthly; you cannot wed
them into vital union. Religion is religion, and
business is business, and never the twain shall meet.
Religion is religion, and politics is politics, and to
try to marry the two is to seek a covenant between
oil and water. You cannot bring religion into commerce, and let the heavenly visitor settle the height
of the tariff wall, or remove it altogether. No, religion is religion, and trade is trade! There was no
chair for Religion in the Council Chamber at Versailles; she was not expected, she was not really
invited. And if, by any chance, she had appeared
and spoken she would have been pathetically out of
place." "But why would she have been out of
place?" "Oh, well, everything in its place; and
Versailles was the place for the stern soldier, the
astute and wily diplomatist, the subtle politician; it
was no place for the saint! You cannot have a
coalition between Christ and Cæsar. It can't be
done!"

"Thy will be done on earth as it is done in

heaven," Jesus Christ said it could be done, and that is the end of it. Nothing is excepted from the heavenly claim. God claims everything. There is no confusion at the heart of things. There is one Intelligence in the universe, one central Will, one great White Throne. God's decree runs through all things, and His holy will is best in everything. What is good religion can never be bad business. What is rotten religion can never be sound economics. What is morally right can never be politically wrong. "Thy will be done on earth!" That is the right road in everything. On that road alone can true life be found, the abiding secret of vital progress and happiness. Then let us firmly grasp the divine principles revealed to us in Christ, let us fearlessly apply them to every sort of earthly facts, let us mould the facts according to the pattern which we have found in the holy Mount.

But let us remember this. These words of our Master are first of all a prayer before they become a commandment. Our hands are to be uplifted in supplication before our feet begin their journey. We are to fall to our knees before we take to the road. It is first a prayer, then a crusade, and then a victory. "Thy will is done on earth as it is done in heaven."

III

TAKING THE HAZARD

"Our beloved Barnabas and Paul, men that have hazarded their lives for the name of our Lord Jesus Christ."
—Acts xv. 25, 26.

THERE is something very delightful in finding these two men bracketed together in a common roll of honour. Both of them are hazarding their lives for the Lord Jesus Christ, and the two men are strikingly dissimilar. Their characters are distinguished by a common loyalty, but their characteristics are strangely different. They are like two musical notes, both of them absolutely in tune, but expressing quite different qualities of sound. In many ways it would be difficult to find two men more unlike than Barnabas and Paul, and yet they both gambled with their lives and put them in hazard in their fidelity to the Lord Jesus Christ.

I am not surprised to have this news concerning the apostle Paul. I do not wonder that he sprang into the thick of dangers as naturally as the stormy petrel lifts her wings at the call of the tempest. For Paul was a born warrior. He was a " bonny fighter!" If a menace arose, or any threat was in the air, his spirit was refreshed. Where is there a record of any antagonist appearing where we find Paul nervously sulking away to his tent? The way of difficulty was always his favourite road. He loved the battle and the breeze. He revelled in close grips with stern wrestlers, and that day was always most welcome that promised a struggle from which he could extort the prize of victory. I do not, therefore, wonder that this man hazarded his life for the Lord Jesus, that he flung himself into the midst of a crowd of adversaries and that he staked everything upon his triumph.

But Barnabas was a very different type of man. I imagine him to be the kind of a man whom we describe as a home-bird. He was more a man of the fireside. He was gentle, companionable, sweet. He was pastoral where Paul was militant. He was the son of consolation while Paul was a man of war. Where Paul would carry a sword, in readiness for an adversary, Barnabas would carry a wallet, filled with oil and wine, in readiness for any traveller whom he might find robbed and beaten on the road. He was a peacemaker, and he was great in the ministry of reconciliation. When Paul would have dismissed a man for cowardice, Barnabas would give him another chance. And so he was greatly distinguished by the softer and more genial virtues. I should not compare him to some splendid cedar, with branches like an athlete's limbs, joyfully contending with tempests on the heights of Lebanon; he was more like a domesticated olive tree, quiet and gentle, laden with fruit, but having its home in the sheltered vale. It was the difference between Jonathan and David, between John and Peter, between Ridley and Latimer, between Gordon and Kitchener. And yet we are told that Barnabas also, the man of pacific virtues, the man who was clothed in softer and more retiring moods, heard the trumpet call of the hour, and hazarded his life for the name of the Lord Jesus Christ. The olive tree revealed the strength and fibre of the cedar. Barnabas and Paul united their dissimilarities in a common and glorious venture. They hazarded all they had. They gambled everything for Christ.

Now, what was it that prompted them to take the hazard? It was the name of the Lord Jesus. They spake of the name where the name carried their fate. Our circumstances are now so different that we have to deliberately enlist the imagination and the historic sense to create the scene, and to give reality and life to the record. I can anywhere proclaim the name of the Lord Jesus, and the name is my security rather than my offence. I exalt it here in this house of prayer, and there is none to make me afraid. I can announce the name of Jesus like a herald in any open square or on any village green in the kingdom, and no menace would darken my steps. The fact of the matter is this—

in this our land the name of Jesus has no religious rival, and when we " hail the power of Jesus' name," there is no contendent for His throne. You can trudge from coast to border, and you can mark the milestones of your pilgrimage by the proclamation of the name of Christ, and never in the entire journey will your life be in hazard, or your safety in peril, or your comfort broken. To merely declare the name of Christ in our day does not in any way recall the circumstances of the early Church.

For, look you, take an example. When Paul went to Ephesus to proclaim the name of Jesus there was another name there before him. " Great is Diana of the Ephesians! " There was a rival on the field. The rival was mighty and predominant. The rival was revered. " Great is Diana of the Ephesians! " And to go into the city of Ephesus and stand up in some public square, and proclaim, " Great is Jesus of Nazareth," was to carry your life in your hands, to arouse the enmity of rivalry, to stir the fires of pride and prejudice, and to enlist against you all the fiercest hatreds of religious passion. To say the name of Jesus where everybody else was saying the name of Diana, was to gamble with your safety and to put your life in hazard. And if some Ephesian, learning the name from you, went along his old ways singing something like this, " How sweet the name of Jesus sounds," or this, " Jesus, the name to sinners dear," or this,

" The name above every name," or this, " Jesus,
the name high over all," what then? What about
Diana? What had that man to face? The pointing finger was outstretched, and the menacing cry
was raised, Yah! Anti-Diana! Anti-Diana! Pro-
Nazarene! If we would know what he had to face
we must recreate and recall the use of phrases
like " Pro-Boer," or " Pro-German," or " Anti-
Patriotic," or " Anti-Loyalist," or any other circumstance where some hoary and accepted tradition has opened the armoury of its terrors, and
marched against anyone who has questioned its
right and authority. In such remembrance we
shall recover something of the mood and temperature of those early days. . . . Well, then, in face
of all this menace in Ephesus, how did the apostles
fare? Let us hear again the simple record, " They
magnified the name of the Lord Jesus "; " They
hazarded their lives for the name of our Lord
Jesus Christ."

It is just here that we may see the intervening
years between their day and ours melt away, and
we may feel the essential kinship between Ephesus
and London. There is now little or no hazard in
proclaiming the name of Jesus. There is no Diana
within our shores to awaken battle. But loyalty to
the name of Jesus is as provocative in our day as it
was nineteen hundred years ago. There may be no
exalted, tinselled monarch who is jealous of our
fine gold, but you cannot maintain your loyalty to

Christ without facing the menace of Mammon, or the irritation of Fashion, or the heavy inertia of Tradition, or the sleepless antagonism of the World, the Flesh and the Devil. Diana has vanished! I said Jesus had no rivals in Britain, and yet these are fierce contendents for her power. The way of Christian loyalty is on that road, the road of open venture. And the all-determining question is this—How far will we go in our religious devotion? What is the extent of our stake? How much will we hazard for Christ? Paul and Barnabas hazarded their *lives* for the name of the Lord Jesus Christ.

For, after all, the real test of the value of our religion is found in the stake which we are willing to wager in the name of our Lord. In one of his books Donald Hankey has a very arresting phrase. It is this: " True religion is betting one's life that there is a God." I want you to notice the nature of the bet. You don't bet your word that there is a God. You don't bet ten minutes or a quarter of an hour a day that there is a God. You don't hazard threepence a week that there is a God. You bet your life on it. That is the stake. " True religion is betting one's life that there is a God." I say that Donald Hankey's phrase is very arresting, and very quickening, but there is not enough life and colour in it for me. I wonder how the apostle Paul would recast and remint the phrase. Most assuredly he would so remould it as to make room for Christ. I wonder if this might be anything like the refashioning: "The true Christian religion is betting one's life that Jesus is the Son of God and the Saviour of the world, and hazarding everything for the honour of His friendship." At any rate, however we may phrase the form of the venture, we may surely say that the Scriptures and Donald Hankey's statement agree in this, that vital religion implies the element of hazard, of speculation, of splendid gamble, and that where there is no risk the so-called venture is dead.

Well, if that be so, we have a ready measure for testing the reality and value of our religious professions. We need not begin with prolonged investigation into the length and details of our theological creed. I have known men and women with a creed as long as your arm, but they had no more spirit of venture than a limpet. Their theology is like a mountain, but they have not the courage of a mouse. Our jealousy for orthodoxy is no proof at all of the value of our faith. What do we hazard for it? The measure of the hazard reveals the vitality of our faith, and nothing else reveals it. It is not revealed by our controversial ardour. It is not revealed by our stern guardianship of orthodox spoils. It is not revealed by the scrupulous regularity of our attendance at church and worship. No, all these may mean nothing at all. What do we hazard for Christ? What have we staked on the venture? How much have we bet that He is alive and King? . . . Twopence a week, or our life? . . . That is the test. Paul and Barnabas hazarded their lives for the Lord Jesus Christ. They staked everything on Him.

Now the New Testament teaches that the heart of faith is venture. If you will study the eleventh chapter of the letter to the Hebrews, that wonderful chapter where the heroes and heroines of faith are honoured and commemorated as in the gathered memorials of some venerable cathedral—if you will study the shining legends of that chapter you will find that every instance reveals a vista of venture. Some man or woman is taking a hazard. Every memorial begins with the majestic prelude, " By faith, so and so . . .," and the sentence goes on to describe a splendid risk. Every emblazoned record preserves the renown of some man or woman who staked everything on the faithfulness of God. You pass from one to another, and they are all the stories of hazardous exploits. They are very dissimilar. In one instance a man is venturously putting himself at the head of a mass movement of his fellow countrymen, and he is leading them out of age-long bondage. In another instance a woman puts a bit of scarlet thread in a window, and risks her life in the venture. Yes, they are very dissimilar. The roads are very different, but they are all alike in the display of a common venture . And therefore do I say, on the authority of the Word of God, that there is no true faith

without venture. Merely to hug a creed and to take
no risk, is no more faith than to hug a time-table is
to take a journey.

Look at it from another angle for a moment.
Let us ask this question—What faculties are in-
volved in the work of faith? Reason? Surely.
Conscience? Yes, surely. Imagination? Yes.
Emotion? Yes, and no; possibly, but not necessarily. You may have faith without emotion, as some
bulbs open out their hidden glory without water,
absorbing from the atmosphere the scanty moisture
which they need. You have all these other faculties at work, and yet faith may still be dead.
Reason, conscience, imagination, may all be present,
and yet there may be no splendid ventures of movement in the life. Reason may perfect her logical
steps and processes. Conscience may become in-
candescent. Imagination may cherish nobler ideals.
Emotion may awake in sacred and chivalrous desire. You may have all these, and yet you may not
have the faith which will entitle you to be honoured in the ranks of those whose glories are re-
counted in the letter to the Hebrews. In those
shining records you see not only reason in logical
movement, and conscience surveying larger moral
issues, and imagination scanning the outlines of
new worlds, and emotion expressing itself in peni-
tential word and tears, you see more than these. In
the faith of these men and women it is *life* itself
that is moving, and it is moving in glorious hazard

and venture. Reason is there, and conscience, and imagination, but all these are vitalized by the vitalizing companionship of the will, and it is the will moving in venturesome journeys. If you have reason, and conscience, and imagination without the will, it is like having three finely upholstered railway carriages, but no engine. They are all right to stand in a station, and you can rest and sleep in them, but they are no use for a journey. Add the engine, and the whole is in movement, and you can go to the ends of the earth! Reason, conscience, imagination—now add will, a venturesome will! It is in the valorous movement of the will, staking everything upon her venture, that life is displayed in the vitality and regality of faith. These heroes and heroines are all in movement, and it is always the movement of hazard and gamble: "They stopped the mouths of lions, quenched the violence of fire, escaped the edge of the sword, turned to flight armies of aliens. Others had trials of mockings and scourgings, yea, moreover of bonds and imprisonment; they were stoned, they were sawn asunder, they were tempted, they were slain with the sword." What wealth of hazard is here! What prodigality of venture! And what is their venture? It is all hidden in this phrase, "By faith!" A risking will converts a passive belief into an active faith. Without hazard there is no faith. Faith without works is dead. Paul and Barnabas hazarded their lives for the name of the

Lord Jesus Christ. They gambled everything on His truth and grace.

And now let me add this word in conclusion. A religion without hazard is a religion which makes no discoveries. Nothing ventured, nothing won! That is the teaching of the world on other roads of experience. It is also the teaching of the Word of God. Nothing ventured, nothing won! Our hazards are methods of exploration, and they are the measures of our findings. No stakes, no winnings! Splendid gambling, splendid gains! What sort of gains? Read what Jesus Christ says about them. What sort of gains? Read what the Apostle Paul says about them. You may possibly remain as poor as a struggling village carpenter, but you will assuredly share the riches of the Son of God. Aye, but there is something even better than that. In the common sort of gambling no one grows richer except the winner. But where a man or woman hazards their life on the Christ everybody shares their gains. All men are better when any man sides with God. He sweetens the world for everybody else. Every noble venture brings Heaven into the common road and makes it fragrant with the perfume of divine truth and grace.

How much shall we put into our religion? What shall we hazard? How much money shall we put into it? Shall it be less than we put on our backs, less than we put into the theatres? How much faculty shall we put into it? How much glory and strength? Shall we toy with it or shall we gamble our life in the business? What shall we put into it?

> Were the whole realm of nature mine,
>   That were an offering far too small,
> Love so amazing, so divine,
>   Demands my life, my soul, my all.

IV

REVELATION WAITING UPON CAPACITY

" I have yet many things to say unto you, but ye cannot bear them now."—JOHN xvi. 12.

THE Master is speaking to His disciples in the upper room. The words are a fragment of the wonderful intercourse recorded for our advantage in the fourteenth, fifteenth, sixteenth and seventeenth chapters of John. If one may make comparison among things, all of which are superlative, one would say that when we enter these chapters we are in precincts peculiarly venerable and awe-inspiring. If one may liken the whole of the New Testament to a temple, then these chapters would be the Holy of Holies, a place where the sanctities are gathered together in overwhelming solemnity and power. In this place things are being said of unutterable tenderness and unutterable grandeur. Their range takes away one's breath. On the one hand they touch human life, with all its frailties, as gently as the wings of a bee touch the stamens of a flower; and on the other hand they lay hold on divine and eternal prerogatives with the majestic air of a King entering the capital city of

his dominions. Christ lays one hand on human necessity, and its touch is as exquisite as the touch of a nurse, and with the other hand He quietly grasps the sceptre of the universe, and He claims the glory of God. Such is the range of movement in this Holy Place, and my text reflects a little of that movement as the great Lover touches the needs of His disciples: "I have many things to say unto you, but ye cannot bear them now."

Now I would not like to say that these disciples were quite ordinary men such as you might find anywhere in any town or village in the land. They were not the first pickings from the street or the shore. They were very carefully chosen. They came from ordinary callings, but I imagine they were extraordinary men. They were not children of advantage. They were not laden with the fruits of culture. They did not carry the influence of lofty rank or station. They had no money behind them which could lend distinction to their weakness. But then their Master had none of these things, and though His disciples had none of them, I still think they were extraordinary men. They must have been men of dormant capacity, and the Lord must have seen the folded secrets of their power. He must have seen the sleeping possibilities which in later years were to develop into a variety of gifts, and into a strength which could carry a message anywhere and boldly face the gathered resistance of a world.

But at present they were very crude and clumsy. They were still in the elementary standards, somewhat dull at taking things in, and their progress in the school of Christ had been painfully slow. If big possibilities were in the bud, the bud had not yet begun to unsheath its glory. And the great Teacher waited for His dull-witted pupils, waited with infinite patience. There was so much to be given, and so little had yet been received. There was so much to be told, and so little had yet been understood. " I have many things to say unto you, but ye cannot bear them now." Our English word " bear " is somewhat ambiguous. At any rate, its primary meaning is that of endurance. When we speak of not being able to bear a thing we suggest some gathering experience which overwhelms us. The experience may be either grave or gay. It may be like a blaze of sunshine, or it may be like a black encompassing gloom. But, whether it be one or the other, we use the word in the sense of " to endure." " I cannot bear it."

But that is not the primary content in the word of my text—" Ye cannot bear them now." In the Master's sentence " to bear " has the simple significance of " to carry." Indeed, that is how the word is elsewhere translated in the New Testament, as, for instance, in the phrase: " A man bearing a pitcher of water." So that when the Master suggests that there are some things which they are not yet able to carry, He means that they have not yet the requisite capacity to lay hold of them and apprehend them. They lack the needful grasp. They may be able to carry a pound weight, but they are not yet able to carry a stone. They may be able to grip this portion of truth, or that portion of truth, but there are other portions which are quite beyond them. It is the grasp that is wanting, and the revelation must wait until the needful grasp is matured. The word therefore suggests the contrast between the hands of a child and the hands of a full-grown man. " I have many things to say unto you, but ye cannot bear them now."

Now the principle is operative in every field of learning, and in every realm of discernment. Revelation has to wait upon capacity, and it has to wait patiently until capacity is grown. A master-musician may say to his pupil, " Music has many things to say unto you, but you cannot carry them now!" Marvellous harmonies are waiting, exquisite refinements of tone, wonders of melodious fellowship, witcheries of cunning combination, but you lack the needful discernment. And the genius of music has to wait until an ear has been acquired which can catch and hold there finer sounds and harmonies. " Ye cannot carry them now."

An art master may say to his pupil—" Art has many things to say unto you, but you cannot carry them now!" There are delicacies of light and shade, there are dainty marriages of colour, there are fairy secrets, there are subtle glories of which you have never dreamed! You can see a little way, but just beyond your range there is a world of gorgeous mystery. And so the spirit of art has to wait until an eye has been acquired which can apprehend and carry the hidden glory. " Your eye hath not seen!" " You cannot carry them now!"

And so it is with what our Lord calls " the treasures of heaven," the higher harmonies of the spiritual spheres. So it is with the finer aspects of truth. They are like the stellar spaces of the universe, crowded with hidden glories, but dependent for their unveiling upon the creation of a more and more perfect lens. With every added power to the lens the invisible world loses a veil, and it displays a new range of its treasures. And thus it is with the truth in Christ Jesus. So it is with the greatest secrets—the hidden knowledge of God and His grace, the mysteries of His will, His cloud-shrouded judgment, the tangle of His Providence —they are waiting for an eye, an ear, a requisite strength of holiness, the needful purity of life. The treasures are even now assembled like the glories of the starry world: they are " the things which God hath prepared for them that love Him," but they are veiled before our immaturity. " I have many things to say unto you, but ye cannot bear them now."

Now let us mark one or two consequences of all this. The first consequence is this: there are many words of Christ which await the approach and touch of adequate capacity. What does our Lord and Master say about His words? This is what He says: " The words that I speak unto you, they are spirit and they are life." Mark the depth of the background which He gives to His words— " they are spirit, and they are life "—and we feel them stretch back, and back, and back, like regions of untraversed and undiscovered country, back and back, losing themselves in misty and mysterious depth. " My words are spirit, and they are life! " They are like unplumbed seas, " the unsearchable riches of Christ."

But let us carefully note that if our Saviour's words are spirit and life, then as we add to the clarity of our own spirit, and the purity of our own life, we are acquiring the necessary means of interpretation, and we can plumb an ever deeper depth in these unsounded seas. It is little or no good coming to the words of life with a dictionary and a lexicon. You can find out something about them, but it is not the knowledge of vital acquaintance. The lexicon may give you certain information about His words, but it no more takes you into the vital secret of His word than the information which " Who's Who " gives me about Lord " X," escorts me into the inner room of his friendship. In the spiritual realm the difference between information and knowledge is the difference between timber and a living tree; it is the difference between the mechanical and the affectional; it is the difference between two callers at your door, a rate collector and a lover. . . . I may know Christ through a scrap of paper: He waits to be known through the wedded and companionable alliance of a pure life. . . . And therefore His words wait for fuller interpretation, they are always waiting for the larger interpretation which is found through a larger life. . . . " I have many things to say unto you, but ye cannot bear them now."

And now we take a step further. If these are words of Jesus waiting for an interpreting capacity, may we not say the same about events? There are happenings in the life of Christ which may seem silent and mysterious as the Sphinx, but the silence is only the witness that the interpreting ear is absent. If only we had a finer ear these mystical happenings would reveal a voice, and the voice would unfold the secret things of God. Events are always insignificant until they are met by the needful power of discernment, and as that power becomes more and more matured the hidden secrets troop out of their hiding like the fabled princes who had been imprisoned in the gloomy wood. What about the happenings in Gethsemane? What is there in them—how little or how much? What about the awful happenings on the Cross? What is there in them—how little, or how much? What about the mysteries of the empty grave? What have they to say to us—how little, or how much? What about the mysteries of the Pentecostal morning? What do they say to us? We cannot stand round these central sanctities of our world, aye, and of all worlds—we cannot stand round them like casual observers, with our hands in our pockets, and with the jaunty indifference of the witnesses of a bull-fight, and yet expect these events to tell us their secrets. Mere observation will take us nowhere. For each and all of us the events are waiting for an interpreting capacity, and until that capacity is presented to them they will look at us, with all the mysterious silence of the Sphinx. These wonderful events have many things to say to us—aye, infinitely more than we dream, but we cannot carry them now.

Well, then, how is this carrying capacity to be acquired? How is this discernment to be gained? Let us reverently consult the counsel of the Lord. The word of my text which expresses our incapacity is accompanied by a word of promise proclaiming how the incapacity may be removed. " I have many things to say unto you, but ye cannot bear them now. But when He, the Spirit of Truth, is come, He shall guide you into all truth." In the Christian life our incapacity is to be leagued with a Guide, who is to be the minister of our spiritual expansion. Mark you, we are not left to an impersonal director—that would be a guide-post. We are not left with an impersonal code of laws—that would be a guide book. The promise is neither a guide-post nor a guide-book, but a Guide. He, the

Spirit of Truth, shall guide you into all truth. And let no one limit the ministry of this Guide to the presentation of knowledge, and to the opening out of secrets as we walk with Him along the way. His guidance is not only to inform, but to inspire; it is to prepare and refine the faculty as well as to present the truth. He not only presents the field of vision, He also intensifies the lens. He creates the eye which is to perceive the scene. He enlarges our capacity, and we apprehend the waiting truth. He guides us into all truth.

And where does He train us? Where is His school? And what is the medium of His training? The common events of daily life. Our faculties are burnished by the smaller loyalties, and we come to see the greater. That is the line of spiritual progress. Our powers are prepared in smaller spheres for explorations in larger ones. We have not two consciences, one for business and one for religion; we have only one, and the conscience is quickened by the hourly fidelities of common intercourse. We have not two reasons, one for secular affairs, and one for devotions; we have but one reason, and it is strengthened by the singleness of its quest through all the jungle of thickly competing interests which throng our daily life. We have not two wills, one for the flesh and one for the spirit; we have only one will, and this will is invigorated by a thousand unwitnessed wrestlings on a thousand obscure fields. Our reason, and our conscience, and our will are prepared in these minor happenings, and they march up to the major happenings and to enlarged discernments.

The heart, which has been tried and proved in heart-break, wanders into the garden of Gethsemane, and wonderingly finds that it has eyes for the darkness, and in the midnight gloom it begins to see. The love which has been trained by the Holy Spirit amid the desolations of wasting experiences, goes and stands before the Cross, and the mystery begins to break in solemn and amazing glory. It is through the guided and inspired ministry of daily events that we thus find the keys to larger interpretations of the word and life of our Lord. The event may be a sunny one, bright as the brightest morning; it may be a little child knocking at the door, God's love gift to our expectant hearts, and the little one brings the key to the very heart of God. Or the event may be a sombre one, cold and black as a starless winter's night; it may be death knocking at our door, and the dark-robed presence is made to put into our hand the key of the grave. In all these ways faculty is strengthened, and perception is refined, and with the increased capacity we are able to hear voices that once were silent, we are able to decipher the meaning of words that once had no significance; we begin to handle more of the keys of life and death. "I have many things to say unto you, but ye cannot carry them now!" Yea, so it is; but when the great Guide has strengthened and purified our powers, then—" Master speak, Thy servant heareth!" And His will and His grace will unfold their treasures to the eternal enrichment of our souls.

For, mark you, this is to be the supreme work of the Guide. He is to prepare our powers for a progressive perception and understanding of our Lord and Saviour Jesus Christ. " He shall glorify Me," says Jesus, " for He shall take of Mine and declare it unto you." Christ is to be more and more gloriously revealed to us through our refined discernments and the ministry of novel and unfamiliar events. Along the great road of time every age should succeed to a larger and richer interpretation of Christ. This age in which we live should see Christ as He has never been seen before—in clearer vision of His truth, in new and broader applications of His will, and in the carrying of His fertilizing spirit to every desert waste in human life. How to know Christ, and how to convert the divine knowledge into human grace and loveliness, that is our perpetual problem; and this is the perpetual solution of the problem—" He shall guide you into all truth, for He shall take of Mine and shall declare it unto you."

We must not be afraid of new things. We must not be afraid of larger ways of looking at old things. We must not fear the new application of Christian truth to the new and complex necessities of our day.   There are two things we must pray for—vision and venture, and for these let us pray without ceasing . . . " Lord, that I may receive my sight."   That is the secret of vision. . . . " Thy will be done on earth! "   That is the spirit of venture.   And vision and venture will translate themselves into venture and vision, and we shall go on from faith to faith, from strength to strength, and from glory to glory.

V

KINGS AS SERVANTS

"And kings shall be thy nursing fathers, and their queens thy nursing mothers; they shall bow down to thee."

—Isaiah xlix. 23.

WHAT a startling figure of speech this is! It is steeped in Oriental brilliancy of light and colour. And it is like a thousand other figures in the Old Testament, very aggressive in their strength, full-blooded things, discharging their mission in almost boisterous strength. What a power of brain and imagination belonged to these Old Testament prophets, and with what decision they married it to equally robust expression! They were poets as well as prophets. They had imagination as well as reason. They had vision as well as sight. And they gave their thoughts and dreams verbal bodies of amazing life and virility.

Look, for an example of all this, at the figure in my text. "And kings shall be thy nursing fathers, and their queens thy nursing mothers." Let us disregard its historical application for the moment. Let us examine it merely as a product of the imagination. What, then, is the imagery? Kings are to put off their imperial purple and to put on the apron of the slave. They are to lay aside their regality and clothe themselves in humility. The sceptre, which is the symbol of rule, is to be exchanged for the towel, which is the symbol of service. Kings are to translate their sovereignty into simple tasks, and they are to humbly minister to people over whom they are supposed to reign. This is something other than kings in mufti. It is power converted into gentleness; it is tyranny transformed. Such is the figure of the text.

And now let us grasp the prophet's application of it. He is speaking to a people who are in exile. They are like the deported captives of Belgium, under the indifferent heel of the Kaiser, and spurned by the imperial militarism of Germany. And what have kings meant to these Jewish exiles? Kings have been the symbols of an alien tyranny. Kings have been the slave-drivers in the bleak fields of their desolation. Kings have been the despots before whom they have marched in degrading bondage. To this disheartened little people kings have meant invasion, captivity, homelessness, exile.

But now a prophet arises among them with power to pierce the immediate gloom of brutal circumstance. He is a prophet of hope. He is endowed with sight and insight. He sees the alluring light of a wonderful dawn. In glowing imagery he foretells their return to their native land. Tyranny shall be ended, and liberty shall be reborn. With an almost gorgeous wealth of pictorial setting he portrays the blessedness of their restoration. The parched ground is to become a pool. The dry land is to become musical with rivers of water. The wilderness is to become alive with the sound of joy and laughter. The desert is to rejoice and blossom like the rose. The old, heavy roads of affliction are to be highways of revelry. The crooked is to become straight, and the rough places plain. And as for kings, those grim symbols of tyranny and oppression, this is to be their fate: "kings shall be thy nursing fathers," nourishing and cherishing the people they had spurned, " and queens shall be thy nursing mothers; they shall bow down to thee." Such is the prophet's imagery, and such is the interpretation of his quickening vision. Kings are to become servants: ancient tyranny is to wear the apron of the slave.

Well now, I am going to suggest that, although we are a long, long way from any circumstances which have any sort of likeness to the condition of these captive Jews, it is not altogether a remote land of legend and dream. I am going to suggest that, as far as we are concerned, something analogous happens on our road whenever our life is governed and ordained by God. There are kingly and despotic things on our road, grim presences which hold us in paralysing servitude, but their alien power is transformed into an ally whenever our life passes into surrendered fellowship with the Lord. The tyrannical kings on the road become our servants, and in vital religion we discover our own sovereignty and freedom. "And kings shall be thy nursing fathers, and their queens thy nursing mothers; they shall bow down to thee."

Let us begin on the outermost circle. Science has laid a firm hand on some despotic kings and she has set them to work as our slaves. For instance, she has harnessed the tyranny of the lightning to the gentle ministries of the garden, and on the plains of Evesham the lightning is the nursing father and the nursing mother of all the fruits in their season. Yes, that grim agent of destruction and death is now quickening the life of delicate growths, and adding stores of vigour to their resources. And what about that imperial presence called Niagara—so awe-inspiring in its eternal flow, so overwhelming in its weight and power? Science has transformed that mighty king into a servant, and he is made to visit distant towns and to light up the homes of Buffalo and Toronto. Niagara's energy is sent on knightly errands to kindle a gentle radiance in the chambers of the sick and the pain-ridden. "And Niagara shall be thy nursing father; it shall bow down to thee." Science has hitched our wagons to stars. She has yoked the tempest to our service. She has captured mighty giants in the material world, and she has ordained them as hewers of wood and drawers of water in the ministry of man.

But there are kings much more overbearing than

these. There are other tyrants on the road, and they drive us about, and knock us about; they oppress us with their ceaseless assaults, and they crush the very life out of us. And it is the marrow of the gospel of Christ that when we enter into the intimate fellowship of God these grim kings become our servants; they bring their strength to our necessities, and so far from pinching us into penury they are made to enlarge and enrich the circuit of our lives. That is what happens when we are in the benign friendship of the Lord. We drive vigorous ministries from age-long tyrannies. Ancient royalties are made to serve us. Their power is transmuted, and we gather our honey from the carcase of the lion.

Let me ask you to let your eyes rest upon one or two of these kings as they pass before us in sombre procession. Here is one of them. What is his name? His name is Pain, and he is a king with an almost endless domination. Every hospital is one of his palaces. Every sick chamber is a room in one of the residences of this imperial monarch. Do you know any home where he has never crossed the threshold, and over the lintel of whose door you could write the amazing words, " Pain is unknown here "? He seems to brook no exception. We are all dragged within his sovereignty, and we are all stamped with the impress of his iron rule. Every wail on the planet is a weird sign of his presence, whether it be the sudden cry of agony, or the moan of a sufferer whom he never leaves . . . I think you will agree with me that, amid all the crumbling thrones and trembling monarchies of our day, King Pain maintains his sway.

Well, what can we say about him? What can we say? We can say this, that King Pain can be so controlled that his tyranny becomes a ministry, that his oppression is leagued with service, and that he is compelled to leave infinitely more than he takes. In the fellowship of God, Pain becomes our nursing father, and his directed and appointed business is to cherish and nourish the precious life of the soul. I do not say that when we become the friends of God King Pain loses his sharp implements; perhaps he does not lose any of them; but I do say that they are not allowed to hack and slash away with brutal destructiveness. The sharp tool is made to carve some exquisite bit of tracery in the essential character of the soul. I cannot say that Pain loses his harrow, and that he ceases to do harrowing things, but I can say that in the communion of God the harrow is not dragged to and fro over the field of our life with absolutely aimless ravage. The harrow is wedded to the ministry of a coming harvest, and it is made to serve the call and needs of the far-off ripening grain. I cannot say that King Pain is deprived of the power of giving pain. He is not bereft of his sword, but it is changed into a ploughshare. He is not robbed of his spear, but it is transformed into a pruning hook.

In the wonderful appointments of God's Will Pain becomes a servant and ambassador of grace, and all he does is connected with a higher purpose which he is unable to defeat.

King Pain is transformed into a nursing mother for the nourishing of virtues and graces. King Pain is made to serve the virtue of endurance until our fortitude has all the splendid strength of an oak. And what else? King Pain is made to serve the virtue of sympathy, and the sympathy subtly widens our discernments until we can take things in which are far away. And what else? King Pain is made to serve the virtue of tenderness, and we acquire that gentleness of touch whose tapping opens anybody's door. . . . And how is all this to be brought about? It is to be brought about in the friendship and companionship of God. There was a man of the name of Paul, who was greatly troubled by King Pain, for he had afflicted him with a thorn in the flesh. " And I besought the Lord thrice that it might depart from me." And did it go? No, it did not go, but it remained in the guarding alliance of the divine grace. " And the Lord said unto him, My grace is sufficient for thee, for My strength is made perfect in weakness." And so the thorn remained. King Pain retained his sway, but it was all directed to the enlargement and enrichment of the apostle's spiritual treasures, and in the fulness of his wealth you and I are privileged to share to-day. . . . Well, then, this is one of the kings on life's road, King Pain. And King Pain shall be thy nursing father and thy nursing mother; it shall bow down to thee.

There is another king on the road. What is his name? His name is Mammon. He has a number of aliases, such as Gold, Money, Property, Possessions, but it is the same despotic power beneath them all. I do not know that any one of us has special prerogative, and is therefore able to complete the journey of life without ever meeting this king upon the way. It is not a question as to whether we are rich or poor. Our relationship to the tyrant Mammon is not determined by our account at the bank. It is not a matter of more or less. One man may have an income of a thousand pounds a week, and he may be gloriously resisting the despotism of King Mammon, while another man may have an income of five pounds a week, and yet be piteously and completely under his sway. If we had the requisite powers of discernment, and if we wished to estimate how far anyone had become a victim of the tyranny of money, we should have to apply a sort of level-test to their life. We should have to bring the soul and the money into the same plane of vision, and then compare their different levels in relation to each other. Which is on the higher level, the soul or the money? Which is upper, and which is under? Which is superior, and which is inferior? What is the attitude of the soul when it looks out upon gold? Does it look up,

or does it look down? Is the posture one of
homage, or is it one of command? It is in this way
that the crucial question resolves itself into a test of
levels, and attitudes, and points of view, and angles
of vision. Where is Mammon in relation to our
souls? Is he on the throne, or is he kneeling at our
feet? Are we his victims, or is he our servant? Is
he our master, or is he the menial of our aspiring
and consecrated will? It is all a question of comparative levels; it is not in any way a matter of
amounts.

But now the peril in the tyranny of Mammon is
this—he never displays his tyranny, and he snares
us into bondage on the plea that he is leading us
into freedom. In a certain very subtle way he
hypnotizes his victims, and in their unnatural sleep
he marches them into his thraldom. Mammon does
not coerce, he allures. He does not throw a cart-
rope around us, and violently drag us into captivity. He inveigles us with cords of vanity, delicate things, silken things, and in quite an air of
festivity he leads us to our doom. We start out on
a gay crusade, but the gay crusade is ere long
changed into a prison. At the beginning money is
our highway, along which we are marching to
something else; in the feverish quest it becomes our
goal. We begin by making money for finer ends,
we end by making money. We make money, and
that is all we make, and we are unmade in the
making.

Such appears to be the tyranny of King Mammon. He hypnotizes his victims, and no Pied Piper of Hamelin has ever had such multitudes in his train. And how he mocks his retinue! Mammon creates desires which he never fulfils. He pleases us with a few flashy adornments while he robs us of our spiritual wealth. He gratifies us with the outer shows of things, but he is all the while consuming our virtue, just as the white ant eats out the inner pith and pulp of great trees, and leaves only the bark, the seeming forms of trees, which a single night's tempest can blow into dust. "Money," says Emerson, "often costs too much." And indeed it does! We gain it at the cost of our moral and spiritual freedom. "At a great price purchased I this bondage!"

Well, what about this King Mammon? All the young folk have got to meet him. I should not know what streets to suggest to you, or by what names they are called, if you want to dodge him. You cannot dodge him even if you would, and there is no reason why you should wish it. Begin all your reasonings about it with one clear word of the Master: "Ye cannot serve God and Mammon." How then? Why, make Mammon serve God! And that is the transformation which is effected when we are living in intimate friendship and communion with God. By God's good grace this despot can be changed into a servant, and he is made to minister to the soul which he aspires to rule. "And kings shall be thy nursing fathers; they shall bow down to thee," and King Mammon shall be among those who bend at thy feet.

Just think of Mammon as a nursing father, nourishing and cherishing all the fledgling graces and virtues of the soul! And that is surely what Jesus meant when He said: "Make to yourselves friends of the Mammon of unrighteousness." What the Saviour meant is this—take My way, and in My companionship, and so compel your tyrant to befriend your soul. So think of money, and so make money, and so use money, that all the while it shall be as a nursing mother with her young—it shall feed and vitalize every offspring of your spirit which makes you the kinsman of your God. There is no more wretched sight on earth than the slave of money. On the other hand, there is no more noble sight than its master. "And kings shall be thy nursing fathers, and their queens thy nursing mothers; they shall bow down to thee."

There are many other tyrannical kings on the road of life, and I must leave you to inspect and challenge them at your leisure. But in all your examination of the royal procession give a good look at one very imperious monarch whose name is Temptation. He is as despotic and cunning a villain as you will find on the road, but, like every other tyrant, he falls upon his knees when you confront him in the presence and authority of your Lord. Give, I say, a good look at him, and study the gospel secrets which tell how to set him to service in burnishing and refining the jewels of the soul.

But let me, as I close, just name another king whose gloomy approach darkens the road as with the fall and pall of night. I mean King Death. Among all the kings on the road there is none more imperious than he. Every movement about him is kingly, even when he comes with gentlest steps. In all the sublime pictures in which Watts portrays the presence of Death, however tender Death may appear, and however light his touch, there is an air of authority and command about him which seems to leave no right of appeal. King Death goes everywhere, and he knocks at everybody's door. "Death lays his icy hand on kings," so imperial is his sovereign sway! He is a mighty king. Is he a necessary tyrant of our souls?

Dare I bring in the word of my text, and look for some transforming light even on this gloomy, dreary part of the road? Dare I look at King Death, then utter this word to my comfort—" And kings shall be thy nursing fathers; they shall bow down to thee?" Will King Death bend his proud back and become the servant of my soul? Yes, that is the sweet music of the gospel of grace. There are some arresting songs of emancipation in the sacred book which suggest that the singers had looked into the eyes of the tyrant and found that his tyranny was broken. For example, here is one believer in the Lord, and his word seems to be filled with something like a taunt, as though he were now playing lightly with an ogre which he feared in early days: " O death, where is thy sting? " . . . What can the adder do without its sting? . . . I say there is almost a triumphant laugh in the taunt. " O death, where is thy sting? " . . . Here is a king who has lost his despotism. He has lost his power to despoil and destroy, and all that is now left to him is the power to befriend the pilgrims he once terrified, and lead them into the sweet intimacies of home, and into the all-comforting love of their Father in Heaven.

Jesus Christ has some strange things to say about King Death. He speaks of him as though, in some mysterious way, his tyranny is so buried in service that the dreadful thing is never seen. Where is King Death in this word of our Lord— " He that liveth and believeth in Me shall never die "? . . . And where is King Death in this word of our Lord—" He that believeth in Me shall never taste death? " . . . And where is King Death in this word of our Lord—" He that believeth in Me shall never see death? " . . . Where is King Death, I say? The secret is here—the tyrant is lost in the servant, and his terrors are swallowed up in the blaze of immortality.

And so it is with all these kings; there is one secret by which their tyranny is broken. There is one King on the road, " and on His thigh this name is written, ' King of kings and Lord of lords.' "

He is the lawful King of the road, and every other
king bows before Him. "Kings shall fall down
before Him." It is in His strong, sweet friendship
that we find the right of way, and every other king
will bend to do us service. King Jesus is not
stingy in His friendship, nor is He stiff and re-
luctant in His communion. The stinginess is all on
our side; the reluctance is in our own wills. "Behold, I stand at the door and knock. If any man
open the door I will come in." . . . "Lift up your
heads, O ye gates, and be ye lift up, ye everlasting
doors, and the King of Glory shall come in."

VI

LEARNING FROM THE WORLD

"The children of this world are in their generation wiser than the children of light."—LUKE xvi. 8.

HOW are these words born in the Master's teaching? They receive their life and colour from the parable of the unfaithful steward. You remember the tenor of the parable. There is a certain man whom our Scotch friends would call a factor, and his business is to administer the affairs of an estate which is not his own. He superintends it for another man, guarding and nourishing the produce, and disposing of it to his master's advantage. He is the telephonic centre of all the instructions which pass through the estate. He is the medium of all its industrial transactions. Much money passes through his hands. And this man begins to hold the money to his own use and profit. He busily seeks to feather his own nest at the expense of the laird. He covers up his embezzlements by the cooking of his accounts. He makes a nice thing of it. And all seems to go merrily, and the trustful laird knows nothing about it. Until one day a very simple incident, almost an accident, just a trifle, acts like a spring on a closed door, and the door flies open, and all the hidden secrets are disclosed. The trusted factor stands convicted of unfaithfulness. He is condemned to render a detailed account of his stewardship, to make good the losses, to fill every gap out of his own resources, and to get out of the office.

Now what shall the factor do? He is reduced to comparative poverty. There is nothing to which he can turn his hands. He has not served apprenticeship to any particular trade. He cannot take to the land, for he has not the physical strength for a farm labourer. He cannot demean his proud presence to the act of begging from door to door. What shall he do so as not to be cast upon the streets? After much thinking and planning he hits upon a bold and ingenious device. He will go round and make friends of all the folks who are in debt to the laird. He will halve all their accounts. "How much do you owe the laird?" "Fifty pounds." "We will make it twenty-five." And to the merry satisfaction of the debtor the bill is made out and the account is settled; and so on, and so on, until all over the countryside there are men who are friendly disposed towards him, and who will at any time offer him the most genial hospitality. "When I am turned out of house and home," he says to himself, "there will be open doors among these kindly folk, and I shall have food and bedding until I can turn about and see my way." And that is what he does. He seeks to secure to-morrow by

adding the most ingenious fraud to those already
recorded in the shameful pages of to-day.

Well, this factor is not an admirable character.
He is fraudulent to the very heart of him. He is
as undependable as a rotten branch. And yet in all
his falsities how nimbly and energetically he uses
his faculties and powers! He brings out all his
mental tools, and he concentrates all the forces of
his will in the effort to save himself from disaster.
He is a rare villain, and he is consummate in his
villainy; he moves in the way of his evil purposes
with a full and undivided personality, every one of
his powers being commandeered to serve his evil
ends.

Such is the factor. And in this parable the Lord
looks at him. He looks at this son of darkness—so
clever, so keen-witted, so alert, so purposeful, so
enterprising. And then He turns His gaze away,
and fixes it upon the children of light. He turns
from the worldly man to the religious man. He
turns from the man whose primary quest is money
to the man whose primary quest is God, and He is
evidently not impressed. " How do *you* fare? "
He seems to say to the children of light. " How
do *you* fare in comparison with the children of the
world? Where is your foresight? Where are
your happy devices? How many tools are you
using in sacred enterprise? How many faculties,
and how much strenuousness are you investing in
the service of your Lord? " . . . And when our

Master had looked upon the one, and then upon the other, He quietly uttered this most tremendous judgment—" The children of this world look further ahead in their generation than the children of light."

Now, what is the significance of this teaching of our Lord? Our Lord is greatly surprised that those who make religious professions do not put as much into their sacred business as other men put into the fraudulent business of the world. And the suggestion of the teaching is this—that He expects us to be as keen, as clever, as ingenious, as creative, and as pushful in the course of the Kingdom of God as other men are in the evil service of Mammon. He wants us to be as expert and as sharp-witted in winning souls as others are in winning worldly gains and favours. He wants us to be as open-eyed and ready in extending the frontiers of His Kingdom as vigilant empire-builders are in broadening the boundaries of a State.

Or, to put it all in a phrase, He expects us to use all the tools in our bag, every one of them, and every one is to be like a polished and keen-edged blade. He would have us make a real business of His business, to be really in it, to be altogether in it, and to be always in it, so that by the fertility and vigour of our enterprise we put the children of the world to shame.

Now let us see how this would work out. I am to bring into my religious life all the faculty and

power which the steward used in his clever life of
disloyalty and sin. I am face to face with the
arduous problems of the higher life. How can I
get into ampler communion with God? How can I
get into a fuller and more prosperous commerce in
divine things? How can I get into a conscious
fellowship with God, which shall be broad, and
deep, and constant, and by what means may the
great ocean highways in my being become crowded
with mystic transports—freighted in one direction
with homage and aspiration, and in the other direction carrying precious cargoes of wisdom and
strength? Well, let me diligently study the unjust
steward, and let me note what faculties he em-
ployed in his successful but ill devices, and let me
employ the same faculties in seeking to enlarge and
strengthen my fellowship with God. What, then,
were the distinctions of this man? I think they
were these. I think he used his reason. I think he
used his imagination. I think he used his ingenuity. And I think he used them all with courage and
decision. And it is the will of our Lord that we
should, in all these ways, strengthen our religious
life, and make it victorious and impressive in all
our intercourse with our fellow men.

Well, then, first of all I am to use my reason. In
seeking to enrich my religious life I am to deliberately think about things. I am to sit down quietly
and think things out. There is a very famous sentence of Matthew Arnold's in which he counsels us

"to think clear, feel deep, and bear fruit well."
Let us take the first part of the counsel, which
Matthew Arnold evidently regards as the spring
and secret of all the rest, and let us think as clearly
as we may about God, and the character of God,
and the will of God, and the things of God. Let
us sit down to the business, and let us give time and
quietness to it. Let us think ourselves on to God's
side of things; let us think ourselves to His revealed points of view, and to His angles of vision.
In the book of the prophet Isaiah, God speaks in
this wise—" My thoughts are not your thoughts."
Well, by the aid and counsel of the Holy Spirit, let
us reverently seek to think ourselves into His way
of thinking, and fill our minds with the divine as-
pect of things. By assiduous thinking we can alter
our thinking, and by changing our thinking we can
transform our lives. " Be ye transformed," says
the word of God, " by the renewal of your mind."

I was in a cloth factory the other day, where they
were weaving the broad West of England cloth.
The factory was turning out different qualities of
cloth, and I was deeply interested in the dissimilarities in the raw material, and in the varying qualities
of the threads as they entered the looms. Even an
amateur could feel the difference as he handled the
raw material, and he could detect grades of refine-
ment in the values of the threads. Change the raw
material and you transform the fabric. And the
mind is the loom in our life, and our thought is the

raw material, and our thoughts are the threads which we weave into ideal and conception, and into finished mental habits and fashions. And O, what poor stuff we weave! What shoddy of raw material we gather together, and what rotten threads go into the loom! Even in our thinking about God our mental stuff is often very cheap and poor, and the poverty is expressed in the fabric and character of our life. Well, let us put in better stuff. Let us change our raw material. Let us raise the quality of our thinking about God and the things of God. That is the very purpose of the New Testament. The New Testament is full of raw material of thought for the transformation of life. But the trouble is, we don't put it through the loom; we don't think it out and think it through. We play with it, we toy with it, as I toyed with the raw material in the West of England factory the other day. We don't think it through. We don't think in a great way of God, and therefore our lives do not become great. . . . This false steward set about thinking, and thinking hard, and in this matter of thinking the children of the world are often in their generation wiser than the children of light.

But this man not only used his powers of reasoning about things, he also used his power of imagination. He pictured himself in the homes of his devoted friends after he had been cast out of the estate. His faculty of realization was enlisted in the service of his plans, and imagination added fuel to his enthusiasm.   And we, too, are to use our imagination in seeking the highest interest and welfare of our souls, and the religious welfare of mankind.   There are two ways of employing the imagination.   We can use it in apprehending the reality of things as they are, or we can use it in apprehending the reality of things as they might be.   For instance, it is imagination that helps us to realize the content of a word which in itself only presents a superficies.   For example, take this little phrase from the autobiography of the Apostle Paul. He says he was " in cold oft."   We can skim the word in ordinary thinking, and we shall no more realize its content than a swallow, dipping its wings in a lake, realizes the depths beneath.   We have to set our imaginations to work.   We have to climb up the long road from the Cicilian plain, and toil over the Taurus mountains in the depths of winter, with a blizzard blowing, and all the time being poorly clad!   " In cold oft."   We are to feel the biting bitterness of the phrase.   That is one use of the imagination.   But there is a second use in which the imagination is used to realize things as they should be.   Here is a sentence which reveals to us a man who is using his imagination in this way: " I saw the holy city, the new Jerusalem, coming down out of Heaven from God."   It was a vision of things as they might be.   By the power of the imagination this man is visiting the Utopia of the Kingdom of God.   Or, take another sentence:

And O that a man would arise in me,
That the man I am may cease to be.

That man is using his imagination in seeing himself transformed and lifted into a heightened life. Now, I think the majority of Christian people do not use this faculty half enough; in many lives it seems altogether dormant. And we are great losers by the negligence. We are purposed by our Lord to live with our ideal self, to rise from our beds with it, to walk and talk with it, to go into battles with it, and to hold on to it in triumph or defeat. See yourself as Christ would have you be, and live with the vision. Get your ideal before you, in vivid light and colouring, a strong, attractive, winning personality," " A—— B——, as Christ would have him be," and let the shining presence accompany you in all your changing ways. It is because we do not see our future eminence and glory that we do not draw it near. We do not use our imagination, and in this matter the children of the world are wiser in their generation than the children of light.

Well, then, thus far have we got in the analysis of this man's character; he did some hard thinking, and he vigorously exercised his imagination. But now, may we not truly say that he put plenty of wits into his device? I am perfectly sure if we had known him we should have said he was an ingenious beggar, arranging, and planning, and plotting, a perfect expert in short-cuts, a past-master in practical dexterities. Everybody knew this man

to be thoroughly wide awake, and they knew,
further, they had to be up early if they wished to
take him in. And it was this wide-awakeness that
Jesus laid hold of, this inventiveness, this subtle
cleverness in devising novel ways for accomplishing
his ends, and He said to His disciples, " If a man
of the world is so keen, so acute, so sharp-witted
in planning contrivances in the smaller warfare of
the world, how dexterous and ingenious the children of light ought to be in seeking the unsearchable riches, and in establishing the Kingdom of
their God! Surely, our Master suggests, of all
people the children of light ought to be the most
mentally fertile, the most prolific in devices, using
all their wits to serve and glorify their Lord.

Well, do you think we reveal such ingenuity?
Do you think we abound in clever enterprises? Are
we very inventive in noble plans and devices as
fellow labourers of the Lord? Let us cast a look
at two or three of these wide-awake folk, and let
us judge ourselves by their standard. Here, then,
is one, and this is what he has to say: " I am become all things to all men, that I might by all
means save some." Do we not feel the sleepless
inventiveness that works behind these words? He
plans this device to win this man, and this other
device to win another man, and this third device to
catch a third man—" that I might by all means
save some."

But for our second example, let us cross from

the first century to our own time, and from Asia
Minor to Harrow-on-the-Hill. John Smith was an
assistant master at Harrow School for twenty-five
years. Perhaps if I just read to you the Memorial
Inscription in the School Chapel you will get to
know something of the man—

To the Honoured Memory of
The Reverend JOHN SMITH, M.A.,
Assistant Master from 1854 to 1880.
Humble, Patient, Faithful, Loving,
To the Young a Father,
To Friends in Joy or Grief a Brother,
To the Poor, the Suffering and the Tempted
A Minister of Hope and Strength;
Tried by more than common Sorrow,
And upborne by more than common Faith.
His Holy Life interpreted to many
The Mind which was in Christ Jesus,
The Promise of the Comforter,
And the Vision granted to the Pure in Heart.

Well, then, was there anything very ingenious
and inventive in the religious life of John Smith,
and in his warfare for the Kingdom? Yes, he
abounded in ingenuities. Here is a sentence which
seems to tell us something: " I like to walk down
Fleet Street," he once said, " where everyone seems
so bent on business that they may need my prayers
to help them." Do you not call that sanctified inventiveness? Think of that strong, gracious personality, moving along Fleet Street, and silently
bringing divine influence to bear upon any hard-
pressed man or woman he might pass on his way.

Many a weary heart would feel a sudden lightening, as if a sweet air from the mountains had visited the faint. They would not know what had happened, but the secret was just here—John Smith had passed by.

Then how ingeniously and inventively he arranged his private intercessions. All was methodically planned—one morning given to the Civil Services, another to the Army, another to Schools and Colleges, another to the Clergy and the Church, and so on throughout the week. He says that in his petitions he used the Army List, " which tells me where my old Fourth Form fellows are now stationed," and Whitaker's Almanack. After all this I am not surprised to read this sentence in his biography : " Of God's answers to his prayers he had no shadow of doubt. They were an habitual experience."

I should say that this son of light was as keen and ingenious in his line as the unfaithful steward was in his. And it is in varied kinds of inventiveness that we are thus to serve the will of God. We are to be splendid strategists. We are to put into our campaign the salt of wit and wits, and infuse everything with a noble sort of sagacity, and a clean and shining sanity. " To draw souls out," says Henry Drummond, himself one of the cleverest and most inventive of all the servants of Christ, " to draw souls out one by one, to buttonhole them, to take from them the secret of their lives, to talk

them clear of themselves, to read them like a page
of print, to pervade them with our spiritual essence,
and make them transparent, this is the spiritual
diagnosis which is so difficult to acquire, and so
hard to practise." But Drummond acquired it, and
he practised it, as I truly well know, and by all
manner of sacred and subtle devices he sought and
found the hearts of men.

And, side by side with this bit of Drummond,
let me put this bit of Charles Kingsley, " I try to
catch men by their leading ideas, and so draw them
off insensibly to my leading idea. And so I find—
shall I tell you?—that God is really permitting me
to do His work." . . . "I try to catch men by
their leading ideas "; that man is a keen fisherman
in life's waters, and by all sorts of consecrated devices he is engaged in catching men. But many of
us put no such ingenuity, no varied sagacity into
our service, and the Lord declares His judgment
that the children of the world are in this matter
wiser than the children of light.

Our Lord calls us to be thoughtful, and imagi-
native, and inventive in proclaiming the good news
of His Grace, and in seeking to bring our social
and national life into vital conformity with the
life and purpose of His Kingdom. Think of all
the daring and multiform propaganda for bringing
the life of our people into conformity with the
devil. Has the organized Church of Christ—the
whole Church—has she no adequate strength and

ingenuity of resource? For instance, can she not get at the truth about things? Can she not unearth things, and explore and expose them? In the word of God she is called " the arm of the Lord "; can she not thrust the arm deep down into the wrongs and perversities of our social life, and rake out the secret crookedness, and then hold that same arm aloft with all the secret things gripped and exposed so as to be seen by everybody? And having exposed, then by the holy grace and blood of Jesus, and by the consecration of every form of inventive sagacity, let us straighten that which is crooked, and redeem and strengthen the lost.

This unfaithful steward, in the service of Mammon and fraud, exercised his reason, his imagination, his ingenuity, his courage, his decision. In the exalted cause of the Lord, and in His holy name, let us also consecrate our reason, and our imagination, and our ingenuity, and let us dedicate ourselves to the service with quenchless courage and decision.

VII

WEATHER-WISE BUT NOT HISTORY-WISE

"And He said also to the people, When ye see a cloud rise out of the west, straightway ye say, There cometh a shower; and so it is. And when ye see the south wind blow, ye say, There will be heat; and it cometh to pass. Ye hypocrites, ye can discern the face of the sky and of the earth; but how is it that ye do not discern this time?"
—LUKE xii. 54, 55, 56.

"YE can discern the face of the sky and of the earth; how is it that ye know not how to interpret this time?" What is the Master's indictment? It is this—these people were weather-wise, but they were not history-wise. They could read the face of the sky; they could not read the face of the past. They could interpret the movements of winds and clouds, but they could not interpret the movements of the human race. "Ye can discern the face of the sky." They had become familiar with certain successions in the natural world. If they saw one thing in the sky they would instinctively relate it to another. When one sort of thing came along they inevitably looked for something else. If a cloud arose in the west, they said, "There will be rain." The cloud in the west had always been the harbinger of the shower. The two always travelled together. They were a married couple in nature, and they moved in fellowship and union. If a wind came travelling from the south, they said, " There will be heat," and their expectation was fulfilled. The two always went together. And thus it came about that these natural successions determined their practice. If the south wind began to blow they took to lighter clothing; if the north wind was about they got out their wraps. And they did all this with perfect assurance. The sequence was certain. The north wind never came laden with fire, and the south wind was never the bearer of snow and ice. They could trust the succession.

How did they know these things? How had they come to be able to read the face of the sky? They had learnt it from experience, from common reasoning, from processes of deduction and inference. Their observation and reasoning had taught them that two things were never found together, the north wind and warmth, and that another pair of things were never found apart, the south wind and the heat. This observation had been so often repeated that at length they came to regard the association as fixed and natural. The observation was therefore translated into a principle, and the principle found expression in daily action. They had studied natural sequences, and the sequences were so constant that they had come to regard them

as cause and effect. The south wind, which yesterday came laden with tropical heat, will not change
its freight to-day and come laden with arctic cold.
The north wind, which a week ago carried the
breath of ice, will not stultify itself this week, and
become the messenger of the sirocco, and scorch the
face of the earth with burning heat. No, the succession abides. The readings are continuous. " Ye
can discern the face of the sky and the earth." The
natural history of yesterday will rightly interpret
natural happenings to-day.

But now Jesus Christ expresses Himself in great
surprise. He is surprised that men's powers of
observation, which are so keen and penetrating in
one direction, should be so dull in another. He is
surprised that while men are so alert in interpreting
one sort of phenomena they should be so blind and
sluggish in interpreting another. The Lord teaches
that these fixed successions in nature have their
analogies in other fixed successions in the lives of
men. He bids the people mark and observe how
things happen in history, what things follow what
things, and to note how the fixedness of the succession is never broken. He tells them to look at their
yesterdays, and at the yesterdays of the race, and
they will find that things appear or disappear in a
very definite order, and the order is never confused.
There are certain kinds of happenings which are as
sure in their retinue as is the certainty that the
south wind will bring heat; and there is another

kind of happenings as sure of their train as that
the north wind brings cold. Look at history, says
our Lord. Observe it closely. You will find that
some things never go together. They are mutually
repellent. They never marry. They never go in
pairs. If you have one of them you may be perfectly sure the other is missing, just as when the
north wind blows you will be sure that the heat is
away. Watch the order of things in history, says
the Lord. Study how they come and go. The
order is constant and unbroken. Read the face of
the past.

And so, in the light of this teaching, human happenings are more than detached events; they are
prophecies and predictions. We are intended to
know, when one thing happens, what will follow it.
Yesterday's happenings should shape our expectations to-day. What has been will be. There is no
caprice. History presents us with certain fixed
successions; these successions prevail to-day, and
we do not alter or delay them by merely ignoring
them, any more than if we ignore the south wind
we change its torrid heat to the cold rigours of the
northern blast. No, history, which is the story of
human experience, records certain definite relations,
and we shall inevitably find these relations are repeated and exemplified in our life to-day.

But the trouble is, according to Jesus, that we
are weather-wise, and we are not history-wise. We
read one face, the face of the sky, and we ignore

the other face, the face of the past. And so we go muddling and bungling along, in private life or in public life, as if, by some strange chance, the south wind will bring a cool breeze from the ice-fields, or the north wind will bring a warm, quickening influence from the tropical home of heat and flame. We act blindly as though yesterday had no fixed lessons. We are dull to historic sequences. We ignore the findings of experience. We turn our eyes from the face of the past. And thus it happens that while we can interpret the movements of the skies we are unable to interpret the signs of the times. "When ye see the south wind blow, ye say, There will be heat; and it cometh to pass. Ye can discern the face of the earth and the heaven; but how is it ye do not discern this time?"

Well, what kinds of fixed successions does experience present to us? What sort of relations are they of which we can say, "This is a fixture; it is as sure as the relation of the south wind and heat and of north wind and cold." Are there any principles which register successions that are as fixed in their processes as the process of nature, and which are as unfailing as the holiness of God? Let me name one or two findings of human experience; they are examples of many, many more, but I think that these seem to be especially clamouring for recognition in our own day. I shall ask if our eyes are blind to their gestures, and if our ears are deaf to their appeal.

Let this, then, be the first example. *History teaches that in all human conflict and controversy no victory is finally effective which does not capture the ramparts and citadel of the soul.* Is that a teaching of experience? What is the teaching again? The teaching is this—we never win a man until his heart is won. The energies of any personality follow in the train of the surrendered heart. If the heart be missed the man escapes. Capture the heart, and you capture the life. I say that this is a succession taught on every page of history. It is a line graven deep on the recording plate of human experience. Have we learnt the lesson? Have we traced that lineament on the face of the past? Or are we ignoring the teaching, and seeking to win folk by some other method than the established one of winning the heart?

Suppose we lasso a man or a people by means of a law, and rope them into legislative compounds, what does history say about it? History says we shall never win them. There is no known succession of that order. The secret of personality can never be seized and held in the leash of a statute. No, we can never by bare law win the heart of anybody, or of any people, whether the people be British, or Irish, or Negro, or the dwellers in the Cameroons. Law leaves the spiritual citadel of man untaken and unpossessed. That is the unfailing teaching of experience.

Well, then, suppose we try another sort of con-

straint. Let us try the finer cords of reason. Very
well, then, let us seek to capture the life of man in
finely woven nets of reasoning. Let us capture him
in the meshes of logic. Let us argue him into silent
fellowship and obedience. Is the man now won?
Has experience any record upon it? Is there any
suggestion in the face of the past to throw a light
upon the problem of the present? Yes, the teaching is perfectly clear. Logic no more reaches and
holds the central secret of man than the north wind
brings heat. Arguments do not storm the central
keep of the soul. Arguments may capture the mind
while the life escapes. That is the teaching of experience. The personality is not led in that succession. Why, my brethren, so far as the religion of
Christ Jesus is concerned, if argument could make
us captive the vast majority of people would have
been enthusiastic disciples long ago. But a con-
vinced mind does not imply a surrendered life. The
reason may surrender while the heart withdraws.
" These people draw nigh unto Me with their lips,
but their heart is far from Me."

Try another sort of constraint. Law may coerce
a man's will. Argument may capture his mind.
The deeper thing has not yet been reached. Let us,
then, attempt a deeper possession by seeking to
wake his admiration. If we can rouse a man's
admiration we are dealing with much finer and
much more vital energies. Law may imprison us
in its restraints and yet leave us cold. Reason may

convince us and yet leave us cold. But admiration
has warmth in it, and the warmth springs from
deeper fires. Therefore rouse the admiration and
you are dealing with more essential things.

But what does experience tell us about this? It
tells us quite clearly that we do not win a life when
we only win its admiration. It tells us that the
soul does not surrender in the line of its admiration. We can admire where we do not love. Ap-
preciation may wander forth while affection lingers
behind. We may admire Jesus and yet not give
Him our heart. An admirer need not be a lover.
That is the teaching of experience. Nay, I think
the teaching is even more definite than that. I
think we are taught that the full personality of a
man never really marches with bare admirations.
You need something more if the really vital thing
is not to be left behind.

" We live," says Wordsworth, " by admiration."
Yes, but Wordsworth does not stop there. Let us
finish the sentence. " We live by admiration, hope
and love," and here we touch the secret. It is when
the admirer becomes a lover that the entire personality begins to move; all its powers become like the
members of a glorious band of music in co-
operative strength, and grace, and harmony. Win
the love, and every current in the life begins to flow
towards you. Win the heart and you capture the
life. It is so in friendship. It is so in marriage.
It is so in the life of a people or a race. Capture

the heart and the castle surrenders. And so this is
our call as this is our crusade; we are to win the
hearts of mankind. We have to think, and speak,
and act, so as to capture the hearts of men. We
have to capture the Irish heart, the Negro heart, the
Hindoo heart, the German heart. Nothing else
will suffice. Anything else will leave us in tragical
arrears. Experience shouts this warning from a
thousand different roads. History records this lesson in every chapter, and on every page. If you
would win a life go for the heart. That is the
unfailing witness of the past. " Ye can discern the
face of the sky and the earth; how is it ye do not
know how to interpret our time? "

And now let me present a second collateral lesson
from the teachings of history. And the lesson is
this—*Material forces can never win moral and
spiritual victories.* Is that perfectly sure? Yes, it
is just as sure as that a wind from the arctic regions
never carries the heat of fire, or that a tropical wind
is not freighted with the frost. Have we learned
the lesson? Or are we deaf and blind to this particular teaching of the past? Do we indifferently
ignore it, or do we believe it? What is the lesson?
Material forces can never win moral and spiritual
victories. Are we assuming that they can? And
does our belief regulate our ways and our manners,
our behaviour in private, and our management of
the state? For instance, in the administration of
our prisons are we assuming that material forces

can win moral and spiritual victories? Are we assuming that an over-aweing carnal power can remake and reshape the characters of men? I freely confess that some of the most miserable experiences I have had in my public life have been associated with visits to prisons, when it has fallen to my lot to go and see men who were confined for crime, whether it were in this country or in the United States. Believe me, everything is frightfully oppressive. You feel the crushing weight of material tyranny, and it holds you like a chain. Everything suggests a brutal sovereignty from which you cannot escape. Everything wears the face of mastery, every door, every wall, every window, every passage, every bar, every lock—everything wears the face of mastery, and it is a very grim and tyrannical face. It stares at you everywhere, and it stares you down.

Well, what are we after? Are we assuming that material forces will win moral and spiritual victories? Then we are flying straight in the face of the teachings of history. There is no such succession known to experience, and we cannot create it, any more than we can make a hard, glaring, pitiless sky yield genial showers of rain. If prison-life is to be remedial as well as punitive, if it is to be the scene of human transformation, other elements must enter into the servitude. And I have seen these other elements at work, effecting the blessed ministry of moral and spiritual renewal. I have seen them at work in that fearfully dismal bastille called Sing Sing, that dark spot on the fair banks of the Hudson, about thirty miles out of New York. When Governor Osborne took charge of that penal settlement, he determined to introduce more humane constraints into the captivity. He would soften the hard material forces with forces of superior order. A little chivalry in the government should touch the wretched victims. And so he set to work. The spirit of confidence supplanted the spirit of mistrust. A little kindness tipped the harsh command. A more genial air breathed over the bleak compound. Wings were added to leaden feet, and discipline was charged with aspiration. Material forces were pervaded with humanity, and the entire life had windows opened upon new possibilities, upon glimpses of better and larger days. I remember one incident as I walked round the prison with the Governor. He put his hand on the shoulder of one of the convicts and said with genuine geniality, " Well, John, and how are you getting on? " The man addressed was " in " for fourteen years. He was a little man, but I think I saw him add a cubit to his stature. And were there any moral and spiritual victories? Was that the succession? Does the south wind bring heat? Does the cloud from the west bring the shower? The moral renewal came with the action of the finer powers. Material forces cannot produce them. A chain can never redeem. A pad-

lock can never convert. An army can never renew.
The material bond can never establish moral con-
victions. Have we learned that lesson? Or down
a thousand roads are we ignoring the teachings of
history and experience? " When ye see a cloud
rise out of the west straightway ye say, There cometh a shower, and so it is. Ye can discern the face
of the sky; how is it that ye know not how to interpret the time?"

What other succession does experience present
to us? Let me mention this as I close—*We release
the best in ourselves when we release the best in
others*. In all your observations have you observed
that staring sequence? One follows the other as
surely as the south wind brings the treasures of the
heat. It is an inviolable succession. When we do
the one thing we accomplish the other. It is a law
of life. And what is it? That when we busy ourselves in liberating the best in others our own best
begins to emerge. We ourselves are more fully
emancipated as we seek another's freedom. We
ourselves are warmed at the fire which we kindle
for another. But do we believe it? Have we
learned that lesson until the knowledge has become
an instinct and a bias in our lives? Are we absolutely certain that when we are enticing some
buried faculty out of its grave in another man we
are cultivating the self-same faculty in ourselves?

For if this be true, let us note the inferences.
Here are some of the inferences. Healthiness

comes from helpfulness. We find ourselves through
our brother. Open out a spring of joy in somebody else and a similar spring begins to flow in
you. Help your brother to find his wings, and
wings at your shoulders begin to play. Nourish
his faith and you gain in spiritual apprehension.
Make a truth more vivid to him and it shines in
your sky like a star. These are some of the inferences. We dig ourselves out of our own graves by
devoting ourselves to the resurrection of others.
Tell somebody else the good news of our Father's
love; tell it them till the music fascinates and en-
trances them, and the blessed harmonies will ring
like wedding bells through your own soul.

Have we learned these sequences? They are the
bequests of history and experience. Do we believe
them as surely as we believe that the south wind
brings heat? Have we really and vitally observed
the successions, and have the observations become
applications in our daily life? What a law of life
is here, a law confirmed by a million of yesterdays!
" Ye can discern the face of the sky and of the
earth; how is it that ye do not know how to in-·
terpret this time? "

What, then, is my counsel to young folk who
have the spirit of inquiry? It is this. Diligently
and prayerfully watch the historic sequences.
Watch them with most searching observation.
Two and two always make four; see what history
has to say about that truth in its moral applications.

Let me urge you to heed these vital successions, to heed and revere them. Be experts in reading the face of yesterday, and bring your reading to interpret the duty and problem of to-day, and then, by the Grace of God, live out the best you have seen, and be more than conqueror in the general life of mankind.

VIII

SALTING THE COMMUNITY

"Ye are the salt of the earth."—MATTHEW v. 13.

AMONG all the other new things which our
Lord gave to His disciples He must have
given them a new material environment.
That is to say, He must have given them a new
relationship to the things round about; and to be
given a new relationship to anything makes that
thing new. I remember being very much impressed
by a sentence, spoken by one of his congregation,
concerning the Rev. Alfred Norris, of Tynemouth.
Alfred Norris was a man of the rarest gifts, and of
an exquisitely refined spirit. He was a passionate
lover of truth and beauty. He had the vision splendid and the poet's dream. His thoughts sponta-
neously ran into moulds of imagery, and every
lovely thing became his willing servant. And this
friend of his, speaking of one side of Alfred Norris's influence and ministry, said to me: " He has
spiritualized the whole Tynemouth shore." His
poetic spirit had taken up one familiar thing, and
another familiar thing, and made them the vehicles
of spiritual truth, until the entire coast-line had
become a sort of mystic literature carrying divine

significance. Alfred Norris gave my friend a new environment; the material thing became his schoolmaster to bring him to Christ.

And is not this like the Lord Himself? He touched material things, and they became transparencies, unveiling spiritual things. Nay, the material became sacramental; the familiar chalice was filled with heavenly wine. He converted common things into spiritual messengers bearing the mind and will of God, until no disciple of His could move about the house, or along the shore, or across the fields, or up the hill, without encountering God, and beholding the mystic light of His Presence.

And here, in this immediate teaching, the Master brings common salt into this mystic fellowship, and no disciple would ever handle salt again without passing through its material portal into a secret of the Spirit. Who were these men and women to whom the Master was speaking? They were men and women who had become His companions and friends. They had accepted Him as the Lord of their life, and by a living faith they are now receiving the vital things of His own Spirit. And so they are really changed and changing folk; the eternal God has made His home in them, and they are being transformed. They are rising into a new way of thinking about life, and into a new way of living it, for this divine Nazarene has mixed Himself with their own personality, and they are re-

newed in the very springs of their being. They are
new creations in Christ Jesus.

And what part have they now to play in the
world? The Lord looked round about over the
restless society of mankind. He surveyed the
corporate life of the community as it was being
lived by the Galilean lake and beyond it; He noted
all its subtle intimacies, and all the vital interde-
pendencies which could not possibly be escaped.
He saw the manifold mixings of innumerable lives,
and all the countless possibilities for good or ill;
and turning to His disciples He said, " Ye are the
salt in all this! Ye are the salt of the earth."
Every man and woman in the company caught the
significance of the word. Salt was used by these
fishermen in sending their fish from the lake to the
market in Jerusalem. Salt was used by these farm-
ers on their land. These shopkeepers and traders
handled it every day. It was the house-wife's commonplace. And they all knew the part it played in
their life. And now they were told that their part
was to be as salt in the world! And all who are
sealed with the name of Jesus are to be as salt in
the world! Their life is to be like salt in the life
of the community. Their thoughts and ideals are
to be like salt amid the mass of current thought and
judgment. Their purpose is to be like salt in the
jumbled purposes of work and play. Their speech
is to be like salt in the daily intercourse. Their
dispositions are to be like salt in all the conflicting

feelings and passions of mankind. " Ye are the salt of the earth." It is the word of Jesus to His first disciples. " Ye are the salt of the earth." It is the word of Jesus to all His disciples to-day.

And now let us get quite close to the Master's metaphor, and let us examine the material thing in our search for some corresponding spiritual thing. What, then, shall we say about salt? What are its qualities? What are its uses? Let us begin with this commonplace: *Salt keeps things from going rotten.* And they had great need of salt in the region of Galilee. The Galilean lake is 680 feet below the level of the Mediterranean Sea. It is sunk like a deep, half-filled cup, with a piece of the cup broken out where the waters escape in the river Jordan. The heat of the cup is intense; the mean temperature is 77°, and half the year it exceeds 90°, and on nearly fifty days it goes beyond 100°. It is extremely difficult to keep things fresh and sweet. Sweet things soon turn sour, and fresh things speedily become rancid. These housewives who were listening to the Master had daily difficulties in their larder, and these fishermen in His fellowship needed to have all their wits about them if their fish was to be saleable when it reached the markets of Samaria and Jerusalem. " What should we do without salt? " whispered one house-wife to another. " We should be helpless without salt," said one fisherman to another. Salt was their splendid ally, it was the strong, pungent antagonist of rottenness. It was the aggressive resister of swift and cunning disease.

And salt gave the Master His metaphor. " My disciples are to be like salt; they are to be the salt of the earth." They are to be the custodians of moral health. They are to be the natural enemies of moral disease. Whenever anything in the life of the community is in danger of becoming rancid the Master's salt must be there to stop the foul invasion. The very presence of the Master's salt must be the pledge of stout resistance. The salt of Jesus Christ must ever engage itself in conflict with rottenness, and it must confront surprise with a better surprise. The lists must ever be set for these combatants—the spirit of salt *versus* the spirit of rottenness, and the salt must always conquer. " Ye are the salt of the earth."

Well, what sort of rottenness is there in the body corporate? Let us take a swift glance at the rottenness whose destructive power is to be opposed and destroyed. The rottenness has many forms. It appears here in one guise, and there in another. For instance, I am just told enough to remember what were called " rotten boroughs." It was a corruption of the franchise. Earlier still the rottenness was of an even more deadly character. The voting power of a constituency rested entirely in the hands of a single man, and if he wished he could sell its representation in Parliament for an old hat or a pair of shoes. The Reform Bill of

1832 abolished fifty-six of these rotten boroughs; that is to say, the rottenness was fought and cleansed by strong and healthy legislation. In later years, which I can well remember, the corruption was of another order. It was the rottenness of bribery. A man would sell his political birthright for a mess of pottage. He would sell his vote to the highest bidder. Anybody could have it for a shilling, or sometimes he would let it go for a glass of beer. There was rottenness in the franchise. There was corruption in politics. Tammany was in the Government. Things were rancid and diseased. There was certainly a crying need for strong salt. " Ye are My salt! Ye are the salt of the earth."

What sort of rottenness is in the community? I saw a phrase the other day in a sporting article which was discussing what one might call comparative sport-values of football and cricket. And the phrase which arrested me was this—" Football has become rotten." The judgment suggests that a fresh and healthy thing has become rancid. And that indeed was the charge. What has happened to football? This healthy-minded sportsman declares that its extreme professionalism has become corrupt and corrupting, and that the sport itself has been almost entirely lost in the feverish haze of the gambler's lust of gold. The " bet " has become far more than the game; indeed, the bet is everything. The spectators are not fascinated by the delightful

skill of expert athletes; they do not follow the game
with mental or æsthetic interest; they are only possessed with the delirious thought that a defeat
means so much money lost, and that victory means
so much money won. The end of it all is not in a
sportsman's garland, but in the gambler's purse.
" Football has become rotten." . . . Rotten! That
is the peril of the house-wife's butter. That is the
peril of the fisherman's fish. There is evidently a
clamant call for salt. . . . " Ye are the salt of the
earth."

I have heard of other rotten things. I have heard
of the rotting tyranny of unfair and unjust laws. I
have heard of rottenness in a man's relationship to
his daily task, rottenness in laziness and indolence.
Miss Lena Ashwell is reported to have said a week
or two ago, " It is a rotten thing in life when people
grudge and hate their work." I have heard of rotten dealings in business. Indeed, there is a col-
loquial phrase which displays its own significance,
" He is a perfect rotter! " It suggests the corrupt-
ness of cunning, the putridity of falsehood.

> What's gained by falsehood? There they stand
> Whose trade it is, whose life it is. How vain
> To gild such rottenness!

I have heard of rottenness in literature and art.
I have known them described as " decadent; "
forces of decay get hold of these vital lovely things,
and they begin to decompose, and to be ill-smelling

and fœtid. " Lilies that fester smell far worse than weeds." I have sometimes heard of rottenness in theatres. I have heard of rottenness in common intercourse, where cynical thought and word can be as sour as sour milk, and where theme and judgment are as corrupt as putrid fish.

Well, all these things are just glimpses of various sorts of rottenness which may infect our corporate life. There was plenty of it about in the time of our Lord, and there is plenty of it about in the world to-day. How is it to be met and resisted? This is the Master's way: " Ye are the salt of the earth." The disciples of Jesus are to be vital enough, and healthy enough, and pungent enough to encounter the corruption and destroy it. They are to confront rottenness in politics, they are to meet it in the realm of business, they are to make for it in the field of sport, they are to be its enemies in the crowded streets of common intercourse, they are to defeat it in the quiet and sequestered ways of art and literature; everywhere they are to provide the antidote to corruption and they are to overcome and destroy it. " Ye are the salt of the earth."

But, mark you, if the salt of Jesus is to be the defence of the community against encroaching rottenness, the salt must not withdraw itself from the common relations of men. It is no good having the fish in one basket and the salt in another, and sending them off to Jerusalem in separate compartments. It is no good having politics here, and religion there, or athletics here, and piety there, and business here and devotion there. The salt must be well mixed with the fish, and Christian discipleship must be well mixed in the general life of the community. The better and the more perfect the mixing the more summary and complete will be the cleansing. " I pray not that Thou shouldst take them out of the world, but that Thou shouldst keep them from evil." That is the word of the Lord. His salt must mix itself in vital influence with all the movements of the common life, and every sort of rottenness must be encountered and destroyed. " Ye are the salt of the earth." It is ours to keep things from going rotten.

But there are other significances in the metaphor which was used by our Lord. Recall another familiar use of salt. *Salt is a wonderful thing for bringing out the flavours in other things.* Everybody who stood in the little company with our Lord knew this delightful ministry. Many a thing remains insipid until salt comes along and awakes and reveals its sleeping flavours. Somebody asks in the book of Job, " Is there any taste in the white of an egg? " Well, no, there is no taste, but a pinch of salt works wonders. And so it is with other things. They do not seem to come to themselves until they are wedded to the salt. It is only when the salt arrives that they become attractive. They were very flat before salt came on the scene, but salt touches them and they reveal a wonderful freshness. Yes, it is only in the fellowship of the salt that they really and truly awake.

" Ye are the salt of the earth!" Thus spake the Lord to the men and women who believed in Him. " Ye are the salt of the earth!" Then are there some stale things, which need to be freshened by the presence of Christian men and women? Are there some insipid things which they could make tasty? Have they the power to awake and elicit hidden flavours that are somehow sleeping in common life? That, I think, is the suggestion of Jesus. Somehow or other the believers in Christ are to be the enemies of insipidity. We are to revive the stale things. The Christian is to move about with a spiritually magical influence which can awake fairies who are secretly sleeping in dingy places, or which can touch a chip of wood and it is transformed into a chariot for the carriage of a king. Wherever the Christian comes things are to revive and reveal their hidden powers.

Just glance at one or two of these insipid things. There is the insipidity of home life. There are some homes that are frightfully insipid. There is nothing tasty about them, no fine flavour. Things are stale and dull. When they want life's flavour the indwellers go away from home. Well, it is Christ's will that when an intimate friend of His is in any home, he or she should be as salt to fetch out the buried flavours. The very presence of a

believer ought to elicit them. Surely we are poor
friends of Christ if we cannot share this much in
the work of resurrection.

And then there is the staleness of the daily living.
There is the drudgery of the common round and
the daily task. How often we hear the phrase,
"Things have become a bit stale?" That seems a
call for the use of the salt! And Christ Jesus says
that when one of His disciples comes where work
is stale and tasteless his very presence should recover some of the lost flavour. Do you not know
people who, when they come into a room, dispel
every suggestion of staleness, and everything begins to revive? And especially is this true when
life has been trodden very bare and hard by a round
of daily cares. Tramp, tramp, tramp! Until
everything has become very flat, and every beautiful thing has gone. It is just there we need somebody whose coming in will recover the lost sanctities. It is just there that we need some presence
whose very fellowship will bring back lost savours
and lost flavours, and release simple and shy delights which, perhaps, have never yet been found.

Do you remember what happened when Dinah
Morris, the saintly Methodist in George Eliot's
story of "Adam Bede," came into the home of Lisbeth, Adam Bede's old mother? Lisbeth was in
sore trouble; she was rocking herself in grief. She
had lost her husband. She was giving a low moan
with every forward movement of her body, when

Dinah Morris came in. " Slowly Lisbeth drew down her apron, and timidly she opened her dim, dark eyes. She saw nothing at first but a face—a pure, pale face, with loving grey eyes, and it was quite unknown to her. Her wonder increased; perhaps it was an angel. But in the same instant Dinah had laid her hand on Lisbeth's again, and the old woman looked down at it." It was the hand of a working woman. " Yes, I am Dinah Morris, and I work in the cotton mill when I am at home." " Ah," said Lisbeth slowly, still wondering, " ye comed in so light, like the shadow on the wall, an' spoke i' my ear, as I thought ye might be a sperrit." . . . " I'd be glad to ha' ye wi' me to speak to i' th' night, for ye've got a nice way o' talkin'. It puts me i' mind o' the swallows as was under the thack last 'ear, when they fust begun to sing low and soft-like i' th' morning.' " Yes, that is it. Dinah Morris was a vital presence who awoke the savours and flavours in the insipid lives of others.

This only must be added about this delicate sort of influence. If you put too much salt into a tasteless dish it does not entice the flavours; it destroys them. The salt must not be too aggressive, or the flavours are buried. " Rather too much salt," we say; which means that some things are hidden. And there is a brusque and self-assertive piety which is no good in the presence of insipidity. It is piety without tact. It is devotion without wisdom. It is sanctity without sense. It is zeal without knowledge. "Too much salt!" The flavours of life do not steal out when it draws near. The flavours are afraid of it, and the tasteless life remains in dullness and insipidity. And so we have this word of the Apostle Paul, "Let your speech be always with grace, seasoned with salt." In the presence of such a vital union, salt and grace, life's hidden essences venture out, and the tasteless days are filled with unfamiliar delights.

I will only add one further word. Common salt neutralizes many a bitter acid. Yes, in the presence of healthy salt many an injurious acid is subdued. And so it is with acids in human life. And what a lot of acids there are about! Acid in irony! Acid in satire! Acid in much so-called wit and humour! Acid in criticism and judgment! Acid in anger and resentment! Plenty of acids about! And if salt is a neutralizer, some of it, and much of it, is greatly needed here.

And that, too, is to be one of the ministries and influences of the followers of Christ in the common life of the world. They are to antagonize the bitterness of human fellowship, they are to neutralize it, they are to destroy it. "Let all bitterness," says the word of God, "let all bitterness be put away." And blessed be God, there are folk whose very presence subdues our bitterness, and changes the acid into sweetness. I think Barnabas of Jerusalem was one of these people. I think Ananias of Damascus was another. I think Lydia of Philippi was another. I think Priscilla of Corinth was another. And such is to be the mission of all who vitally believe in Jesus Christ and share His life. Their salt is to counteract the prevalent acids and change a destructive bitterness into genial sweetness.

But, " if the salt have lost its savour! " Aye, indeed, and what then? If the salt have lost its power, what then? When saltless salt touches rotten things, how then? When saltless salt touches insipid things, how then? When saltless salt touches bitter things, how then? " If the salt is saltless," says the Master, " it is thenceforth good for nothing but to be cast out and trodden under foot of men."

" Have salt in yourselves! " So speaks the word of God. Aye, but how and whence? " Have salt in yourselves." The vital salt is Christ's own life. It is His very Spirit. It is His very Self. And only as the very salt of Christ dwells in us are we able to salt society. Apart from Him we can do nothing. In Him we have the very salt of life, and only as we abide in Him are we able to salt mankind.

IX

THE EXPLOITS OF THE FAITH

"Out of weakness were made strong, waxed valiant in fight."—HEBREWS xi. 34.

THIS is surely one of the most wonderful chapters in the Bible. As literature alone it has all the force, and rhythm, and dignity of an army marching with banners and bands. Or shall we call it the Westminster Abbey of the Scriptures? Its massive and yet exquisite setting provides a hallowed shrine for the heroes and heroines of the faith. You move around the stately pile, and you read the monumental eulogies which record the valiant doings of the soldiers of the Lord. Here are Abel, and Enoch, and Abraham, and Isaac, and Jacob, and Joseph, and Moses, and many others whose names and triumphs are inscribed in this majestic scriptural Abbey of courage and devotion. They are all conspicuous members of a noble army. Their warfare was fought on very varied fields. They are gathered from many centuries. But they had one cause, and they carried one banner, and they sought the honours of one Lord, and they covered themselves with distinction, and together they share the eternal glory.

Yes, I think we may call the chapter the Westminster Abbey of the Bible, erected to the immortal
glory of the soldiers of the faith.

I have used the words valour, and courage, and
glory, and these words call to my mind the armies
of Europe, and the marvellous warfare which very
recently possessed the whole of our Continent. I
recall the features of that warfare; the conviction
that lay within it, the courage that marked it, the
endurance, the self-forgetfulness, the self-sacrifice.
And then I turn my eyes upon the army of the
Lord, and I ask whether the soldiers of Jesus are
distinguished by the same valour, and the same
glorious abandon, and the same ready and joyful
sacrifice. What is the quality of the soldiers who
have been born and bred in the army of the Lord?
Is there anything of sacrificial blood in their intercessions, in their beneficence, and in their service?
Here is a book we call the Acts of the Apostles,
and this book is blood-red from end to end. There
is nothing cheap and bloodless in its happenings.
Every event is stamped with sacrifice. Everywhere
and in everything men and women are giving their
blood.

But is the books of the Acts of the Apostles only
a remote record of an early day? Is it now only a
dim reminiscence of a dead and buried world?
Were those early apostolic labourers the only witnesses who have washed their robes in the blood of
the Lamb? Nay, rather, my teaching shall be this,

that new chapters are even now being written in the Acts of the Apostles, and that every year of our modern life adds to the shining record! The apostolic exploits can be matched in modern missions, and the last fifty years are as rich in sacrifice as the first wonderful fifty years which followed the resurrection of our Lord. Take any event you please in the Acts of the Apostles, which is fragrant with grace, and noble in valour, and I will engage to find its glorious and blood-red counterpart in the annals of our own time. And my simple purpose is to look at some of the early missionary soldiers of the Cross, who are revealed to us in the Acts of the Apostles, and then to put into the same ranks with them, to march abreast with them, unabashed and unashamed, some of the warriors of our own day. This is not the presentation of an abstract argument for Christianity; it is the compelling reasonableness of actual life, and it is, therefore, a superlative argument for the sustaining and triumphant energies of divine grace.

Where, then, shall I begin? Let us begin with the first martyr, the apostolic missionary, Stephen, "a man full of faith and of the Holy Ghost." I want you to fix your eyes upon Stephen in the moments of his martyrdom. He has just been making a mighty confession of Christ as the Saviour of the world, and the hostile Jews were incited to the frenzy of a mad antagonism. "They ran upon him with one accord, and cast him out of the city, and stoned him." And you know how, in the midst of that brutal death, the superb courage of this soldier emerged and expressed itself in the tenderest self-forgetfulness, and in the gentlest and most chivalrous benediction: "And he kneeled down, and cried with a loud voice, Lord, lay not this sin to their charge!" What loftier form of courage can you conceive than the courage which dares to be gentle to the brutal, and which ministers kindly to those who are the ministers of death? The courage which attends to the wounds of the bruiser is the very valour of the Lord.

Well, now, can it be matched in our own day? Have we any missionaries on the field who have blood enough to reveal this sacrificial courage? Have you read of the doings of the Kurds in and around the city of Urumia? The record constitutes one of the blackest chapters in all the black records of the apalling war. The brutality of the Kurds has been unspeakable. "One of the cases reported was that of a girl of twelve who was taken to a life of slavery. The mother protested, and tried to save her child, who was ruthlessly torn from her. As the daughter was being dragged away, the mother made so much trouble for her oppressors, and clung to them so tenaciously, that they stabbed her twelve times before she fell, helpless to save her little girl from her awful fate." "The American missionary stood almost alone for more than a year in this city of Urumia. No con-

sul; no foreign resident; no outside help." Alone!
And now we are ready for a sentence from a letter:
"Another great privilege of these days was the
opportunity to serve dozens of Kurds who needed
medical help!" My God! what strong and tender
chivalry! What self-forgetful chivalry, ministering to the wounds of those Kurds that they might
win their hearts and woo them into the love and
grace and peaceableness of the Lord Jesus Christ.
I say, does not this match the gentle valour of the
early day?

Go back a little way. James Hannington, the
first Bishop of Eastern Equatorial Africa, was
murdered by the people whom he sought to redeem.
Let me give you the last entry in his journal.
"Eighth day in prison, I can hear no news, but I
was held up by Psalm 30, which came with great
power." Perhaps you would like to be reminded
of the nature of this Psalm. It is a singing Psalm,
full of holy triumph, and one of its closing verses is
this: " Thou hast turned for me my mourning into
dancing: thou hast put off my sackcloth, and girded
me with gladness." The next day the good Bishop
was slain by the spear of a treacherous native, and
he became numbered with the glorious army of
martyrs.

Now mark the magnificent sequence. Bishop
Hannington's son offered himself for service on the
field on which his father was slain. He went and
laboured among the very men who had sought his

father's blood. His father's murderer was dead, but with all the ardour of a hound of the Lord he sought the soul of the murderer's son, and he won him for Christ, and he baptized him into the Christian faith as he made the open confession of the Saviour's name. I dare to place this modern record side by side with the gentle chivalry of the Apostle Stephen, and the modern record is not dimmed!

Let us turn again to the apostolic record, and let it be to an incident which is very quietly told, with no exclamation mark, and with nothing to suggest that anything unusual has taken place. The Apostle Paul is in Lystra, busy night and day in gracious and beneficent service, telling the story of grace, and restoring a cripple who had never walked from his mother's womb. And on the very day of this chivalrous ministry a hostile crowd gathered, and " they stoned Paul, and drew him out of the city, supposing he had been dead." What then? The beaten and broken Apostle came to consciousness again. What then? Let me read the Word: " And he returned again to Lystra." That sentence always makes my heart leap with its exaltation of a quiet but magnificent heroism! Back to the place of the stoning, as though no stoning had taken place! He was black, and blue, and sore, and broken, and weak and burdened with loss of blood. But he returned again to Lystra, to tell them about Jesus, and the story of redeeming grace and love. What is there which happened in the European war which can make that courage look pale and dim?

But can this scriptural record be matched in our own time, or is it one of the brilliant exploits of a dead and bygone day? I turn your thoughts to James Chalmers, the noble pioneer missionary to New Guinea. I cannot stop to tell what perils, and hardships, and awful deprivations this man endured to tell the natives of New Guinea of Jesus and His love. There were long seasons of his tremendous ministry when he could have truly said with the Apostle Paul, "I die daily." When he had been out for twenty-one years, nine of them spent in the island of New Guinea, he was induced, after much constraint, amounting almost to compulsion, to come home to rest. I met him when he returned, one of the most arresting and splendid personalities I have ever seen. He stood up there in London, on the platform of Exeter Hall, and in the course of a driving speech he used these words: " Recall the twenty-one years, give me back all its experience, give me its shipwrecks, give me its standings in the face of death, give it me surrounded with savages with spears and clubs, give it me back again with spears flying about me, with the club knocking me to the ground, give it me back, and I will still be your missionary." Yes, and we gave him back to the field. He returned again to his Lystra, and this gloriously brave and leonine apostle of the Lord laid down his life and won the martyr's crown.

" Give it me back," he said, " and I will still be your missionary."

Have we forgotten Father Damien? His life is well within my own life, and his story matches any record in apostolic days. If the author of the Epistle to the Hebrews had been writing his letter to-day he would have given Father Damien a niche in his Westminster Abbey with the other heroes and heroines of the faith. Father Damien sailed out of the beautiful harbour of Honolulu in company with fifty banished lepers, to spend the rest of his days on the leper island. " Now, Joseph, my boy, this is your life work," he said to himself, as he scrambled on shore and saw the other leper inhabitants awaiting him. " Half clothed, ragged, and dirty, many of them with faces stained and scarred, sometimes almost shapeless with the ravages of leprosy, with hands and feet maimed and bleeding, mortifying limbs and decaying flesh, there they were gathered together in ghastly groups; and these were the most healthy inhabitants of the island; the more helpless and dying were lying in the settlement two or three miles away." Father Damien lived a life among them of the uttermost sacrificial labour. He so identified himself with the people that in all his letters his customary address was " we lepers! " He often carried the dead in his own arms to their graves. Ten years passed, and then the great hero saw in himself the symptoms of leprosy. He was still cheerful, and felt the

lepers to be nearer and dearer to him than ever.
And now comes the sentence that burns in my mind
like holy fire, and blazes alongside the words of
James Chalmers which I have just read to you.
*" I would not be cured if the price of my cure was
that I must leave the island and give up my work!"*
What quality do you assign to courage like this?
In his Lystra Father Damien took the leprosy, and
he would not leave his Lystra even for the priceless
bounty of a perfect cure. What is there which puts
that valour to shame? It is surely one of the blood-
red marks of the Lord Jesus.

· But strong and massive virtue is not always of
the scarlet order, nor does it always robe itself in
quieter khaki. The finest virtue is often dressed
in the plainest and most unobtrusive gray. I have
been unveiling some very brilliant virtues; now
let us look at one of a homelier but equally sacrificial order. Let me turn again to the Acts of the
Apostles: *" And Paul continued in Corinth a year
and six months teaching."* And this is all we know
about that year and six months. He was just teaching ignorant people, and there is nothing in the
work that calls for particular record. But how
tame, and gray, and unadorned! Just teaching
people about Jesus who find it difficult to learn!
Yes, but what powers of endurance it needed, and
what resources against weariness, and what springs
against drought, and what inspirations against retreat! We have seen the great Apostle robed in

scarlet courage; here he is in the plain gray of a perseverance that will not be bored, in the plain gray of a pertinacity which no glittering snare can entice from its road. I am perfectly sure that in the scriptural Westminster Abbey, and among the heroes and heroines of the faith, there are niches for those who wear the quiet gray of obscure and unapplauded perseverance. It is the illimitable patience of secret and unregistered labour. It is the quiet but prolonged dripping of sacrificial blood.

In 1914 I was in Beirut. One of the main things I wanted to see in that fascinating town was the printing-house where the Bibles are printed which are sent out to every part of the Moslem world. I walked about among the machinery. I handled the very type with feeling of reverence. There is a great worker for God in that place, and he was busy on the marginal references of the Moslem Bible. And the Arabic letters are so delicate, and so complicated, and the pointing is so minute and the work is so scrupulous and almost microscopic that we found this hero of God, Dr. Hoskins, was beginning to lose his sight. For twenty-eight years he has been working away at the Moslem Bible. Nothing scarlet about it, not even khaki courage, but the magnificent gray courage which can pass the breaking point and not break, and go gloriously on with its task, having no spectator but God. And so do I put Dr. Hoskins in the rank with

Father Damien, and both of them in the brave company of the Apostle Paul.

If you went to Canton you would see a home and school for the blind. You would find two hundred blind boys and girls. Many of the little girls, indeed almost all of them, have been rescued from an unnamable slavery into which they had been sold by their parents. One little sentence in the report reads thus: " None of these girls came from homes." That brief word is significant of horrors far more terrible than the horrors amid which Father Damien lived and died. There is a noble woman in that home who has been working in this blessed ministry for thirty-four years. Send your imagination working down that long lane. What a glorious tenacity of mighty Christian purpose! What resource of plain, home-spun perseverance! What invincible courage! On, and on, and on, and on; just a plain road without a banner and without a band. Thirty-four years! I take off my hat to this glorious worker on the battlefield of Canton, who for thirty-four years in the army of the Lord has just been bleeding away in quiet, sacrificial and blessed ministry for these blind and orphaned slave-children for whom our Saviour died.

Yet all these are but typical examples which might be indefinitely multiplied. Take any exploit you please from the Acts of the Apostles. It can be matched in the story of modern missions. The songs which were sung in the hour of tribulation can be matched by the midnight songs of our own time. The courage which was placarded in the presence of fierce persecution in Jerusalem and in Asia Minor can be matched by the courage of persecuted Christians to-day. The Acts of the Apostles is still being written, and dazzling chapters are being added in the shining record of the missionary life of to-day. Christ has heroic men and women at the front, soldiers of the Cross who are exhibiting as cool a nerve, and as noble a courage, and as tenacious a patience, and as gloriously extravagant a sacrifice, as any which you could have found in the battle-trenches and hospitals of Europe. But what about ourselves? Are we in the field or out of it? Are we soldiers, or only spectators? Nay, are we really less than spectators, not sufficiently interested even to turn our eyes upon the glorious war? How much do we care for the salvation of the world? Our sons have given their blood for the defence of the Fatherland, and for the sacred cause of liberty, and for the honour of the plighted word. What are we ready to give for the glory of our Saviour, and for the extension of His Kingdom of righteousness and peace? If all the soldiers in the army of Jesus gave themselves and their money to the service of the Lord, with the same glorious abandon as our men gave themselves to the warfare of the flesh, we should speedily engirdle the globe with the evangel of grace, and we should create heavenly airs in every land in which the devils of hatred and jealousy would be unable to breathe. Shall we do it? In this stricken and appallingly war-swept world the blessed Saviour is calling. He is calling for men and women and munitions and money. Shall we refuse Him? I appeal to every reader, young and old—nay, the Master Himself appeals to us to have a share in His holy and glorious campaign. Let us give ourselves to our Lord in the uttermost consecration. Let us give Him our spirits in ceaseless intercession. Let us give Him our strength in the readiness of exultant service. Let us give Him our money in most joyous and bountiful beneficence. Let us give to the point of blood, and let us know the joys of sacrifice. Let the angels in glory be constrained to whisper to one another: " They bear the marks of the Lord Jesus."

X

UNTO THE HILLS

I will lift up mine eyes unto the hills.—PSALM cxxi:1.

I SUPPOSE everybody has a sort of hill-country in their life. I mean that in every lot there is a place where indifference rises into desire, a place where the dead level of monotonous concerns towers in aspiration and ambition. I cannot conceive of a life where the entire territory is like an unchanging and uniform plain. Somewhere every life rises into wish, and hope, and admiration. It may be that the hill-country in a life is only a low and unimpressive range, or it may be that it rises into vastnesses of radiant glory. It may be that the high land is only the little hill which John Bunyan calls Lucre, with its silver mine, and which lured so many pilgrims to their perdition. Or it may be that the attractive range is found in those other heights which Bunyan unveils to us, those heights of Beulah-land, where the birds sing continually, and the flowers appear, and the sun shines night and day. Yes, the hills may be of varying order, as widely different as the rugged Rockies and the sweet green heights of the Lowlands of Scotland. But every life has its hill-country to

which the soul looks up in hearty longing and in
eager quest. And it is a great thing to find a life
with a great and noble range, its heights of desire
as pure as snow-clad Alpine peaks on which are
born rivers of beneficent energy which quicken and
fertilize the fields of the plain.

Now, it is a very happy, and also a very serious
and responsible prerogative in life that we can
choose our mountain ranges, and our lives can face
and approach them in progressive admiration and
hope. It may be helpful if I name two or three
superlative heights which I think ought to be in
everybody's hill-country. They are venerable with
history. They are rich in proffered bounty. They
have all the arresting glory which always dis-
tinguishes the hills of God. And the first hill which
I will name is the *hill called Sinai*. Sinai ought to
form part of the landscape of the soul. It is a
majestic height. It is cloud-capped, and veils of
mist swirl about it slopes. It is the hiding place of
mystery. Out of its dark, secret depths there came
the divine voice, uttering God's holy will in the ten
Commandments. Sinai was the birthplace of the
moral law. It was in the sombre testing of Sinai
that the moral order was imposed upon chaos. It
was on Sinai that licence was supplanted by freedom. Sinai stands for the conquest of anarchy. It
is an august height, and thunder and lightning play
round about its cloaked summit. It is described in
the Word of God as "a mountain that burned

with fire," " the home of blackness and darkness
and tempest, and the sound of a trumpet, and the
voice of words." Sinai proclaims the law of the
Lord.

Well, now, that wonderful peak must be in our
mountain range. Sinai has not crumbled away to
the plain. Its commandments are not the ghostly
whispers of a dead world. Its august decrees have
not lost their virtue like some system which has had
its day and ceased to be. The ten Commandments
are not interesting curiosities for some antiquarian
museum. Not one single charge in all their charges
has been abrogated. They are as authoritative to-
day as on the day when the sound of their proclamation broke the age-long silence of the desert.
They are as modern as the Parliamentary legislation of last session, and they are far more imperative. And, therefore, do I say, that when we lift
up our eyes unto the hills, Sinai must be one of the
hills, and it must lay its impressive moral sovereignty upon the entire landscape of our life. What
think ye? Is there any need of Sinai in our personal life? Is there any necessity for the urgent
pressure of the ten Commandments? When we
put them on one side recall what happens. Think
of the expediencies to which we resort. Think of
our moral compromises. Think how subtly we
wiggle out of obligation. Think of the nature of
our excuses. Think how easily we make the worse
appear the better reason. Think how cunningly we

can dress up duplicity, and how daintily we can throw an altar cloth round about a falsehood. It is perfectly amazing, when the moral light is turned down, how skillfully we can juggle with things. I remember some time ago seeing a very attractive looking Bible, and when I turned to open it I found it was a cash-box. Which thing is an allegory of many other things. We can give worldliness a very pious appearance. We can throw a sort of priestly cloak about a deed which goes forth to devour a widow's house. We can be amazingly expert in diluting moral obligation and mixing wine with water. We can betray our Lord with a compromise. Aye, there is a way of selling an article which at the same time sells the Lord. When the moral light burns low, vices begin to parade as virtues, and it may come to be that we are scarcely aware of the delusion.

And, therefore, it is a mightily disturbing and invigorating influence to get near this mountain called Sinai, and to stand before the Lord. There is something profoundly correcting in standing there alone and letting the ten Commandments ring their solemn decrees in our attentive and receptive ears. As we stand there, listening to the Commandments, moral compromises are ripped asunder like cobwebs in a tempest. I do not know anything which would just now be more healthy than the solemn introduction of the ten Commandments into the parlour, into the club, into the counting-

house, into society. " Thou shalt not bear false
witness against thy neighbour." " Thou shalt not
steal." " Thou shalt not commit adultery." It is
a great and a deepening thing to lift the eyes upon
this hill called Sinai and to listen to its bugle speech.
Sinai lays a strong grip upon our chaos, and it
transforms loose compromise into noble decision.

And, surely, if Sinai is needed to-day in personal
life it is equally needed in corporate life. There are
morally anarchic influences ravaging society. The
imperative of the moral law is flouted as a myth.
The anarchy is touching marriage with its defile-
ment. It is desecrating the family. It is dissolving
every kind of sacred bond. It is dishonouring
covenants. It is unloosening the sanctity of speech.
It is laughingly decrying the necessity of worship.
We have been forgetting Sinai, and I am afraid
that the hill called Lucre, with is silver-mine, has
been taking its place. And, therefore, I am plead-
ing that, in personal and in national life, Sinai be
re-established in the mountain range of our ideals.
Sinai is the sublime height of moral law. Sinai is
the proclamation of God's most Holy Will. " Thy
righteousness is like the great mountains." " I will
lift up mine eyes unto this hill, from whence cometh
my help."

But I could not advise anybody just to have the
hill called Sinai in front of their door. Judging
by the knowledge of my own heart, and from the
experience and testimony of others, to live with

Sinai only is to have an oppressive and terrifying companion. And we are not intended to do it. There is another height in God's wonderful mountain range which is intended to be the complement to Sinai, and the second takes away the paralysing terror from the first. And the second hill is the *hill called Calvary*. I do not think that either hill is intended to hide the other. Shall we rather say that each can be better apprehended in the light of the other? Sinai is the proclamation of law. Calvary is the proclamation of love in which that law is fulfilled. I think it is quite impossible to express the amazing difference between Sinai and Calvary, for human speech can no more hold the wonder than a cockle shell can hold the Atlantic floods. But those who are familiar with both heights delight to use even the faulty instrument of speech in lame attempts to make known their discoveries. And wonderful things are told us about the two mountains, and the most wonderful is this —that He who gave the law on Sinai is on the Cross at Calvary. On Sinai God speaks in words. On Calvary God speaks in stupendous act. Let us try to feel the difference.

Go back to Sinai. On Sinai we have most vivid Commandments. It is the vividness of a searchlight. Nay, it is not so much light as lightning. It is terrific rather than pacific. There is little genial warmth about it. There is very little of comfort and little of sunshine. Sinai is very austere. There are no flowers about. Sinai is law without grace. It is decree without promise. Its commandment is more a cold guide-post than a friendly guide. Sinai is very impersonal. God is in hiding. Only His voice is heard.

But look again. On Sinai God is commanding; we do not see Him suffering. He makes known His will; He does not reveal His heart. We see His antipathy to sin; it blazes before us; we do not see His sympathy with the sinner. Can God grieve? Sinai has no answer. Can God suffer? Sinai has no answer. Can God weep? Sinai has no answer. Can God love? Sinai has no answer. And if we have broken the commandment of Sinai, and broken it again and again, and if we ourselves are broken in the breakage, we do not meet any winsome face of healing reconciliation when we turn our face to the mist-covered mountain. Sinai has no amelioration. Sinai has no cordials, no antidotes, no balms. We are broken, and over the blackness of Sinai there shines no star of hope.

We must turn to the second hill, the hill called Calvary. On Sinai we see God's holy will; on Calvary we see the sacred heart. On Sinai law is enthroned; on Calvary grace comes down our souls to meet, and glory crowns the mercy seat. I do not take the burden of my sin to Sinai. I do not know the way. I have not heard of its healing springs. And indeed I am not invited to take my burden to Sinai; the invitation comes from Calvary where

the veil is lifted upon infinite love. On Calvary we
have the amazing spectacle of a suffering God, and
in His sufferings we find the springs of our forgiveness. We ought never to grow coldly accus-
tomed to this wonderful news. Calvary ought to
throw us into new surprises every time we see it,
and every time we hear its story. God weeping is
infinitely more wonderful than God speaking. God
suffering is infinitely more awful than God punish-
ing. God on the Cross is infinitely more amazing
than God on the throne.

Will you pardon a personal reference? It concerns a memory of my boyhood that has never lost
its colour or its strength. It is the memory of my
mother reproving me in tears. Punishment might
have been bearable but I could have faced it. But
tears, they vanquished me! A mother's suffering
for a son's disloyalty to truth—there was something in that which made my act repulsive and at
the same time unveiled to me a heart of love and
reconciliation and peace. May I not ascend by that
little human slope of filial experience to the Cross
of my Lord on the hill called Calvary? There our
God unveils our sin, and there He unveils the love
which forgives the sin and can redeem the sinner.
Sinai has no place for sinners, Calvary has no place
for anybody else. There we can take our burden
and we need never bring it away. " Now I saw in
my dream that Christian ran till he came to a place
somewhat ascending; and upon that place stood a

Cross, and a little below, in the bottom, a Sepulchre.
So I saw in my dream that just as Christian came
up with the Cross, his burden loosed from off his
shoulders, and fell from off his back, and began to
tumble, and so continued to do, till it came to the
mouth of the Sepulchre, where it fell in and I saw
it no more. Then was Christian glad and light-
some, and said with a merry heart, ' He hath given
me rest by His sorrow, and life by His death.' "
Sinai means the proclamation of law and the conquest of anarchy. Calvary means the proclamation
of love and the conquest of sin. Sinai is the voice
of a trumpet exceeding loud. Calvary is the voice
of love and mercy, the evangel of redemption. " I
will, therefore, lift up mine eyes unto this hill from
whence cometh my help."

There is a third hill that must fling its beneficent
influence upon our life. I can face anarchy in the
intense light of Sinai. I can face sin in the tender
reconciling light of Calvary. But there is another
terror upon my road. His name is Death. Havoc
is in his hand. He is a spoiler, and he seems to
ruthlessly rend the loveliest vesture of human fellowship. A life may be sweet and whole as a
beautiful garden, and then in the garden death
makes a grave, and somehow or other the grave
appears to fill the garden. If the grave were the
goal of things, if it were the end of love and of all
noble endeavour, the game would not be worth the
candle. And there he is, the Terror! I cannot

escape him.   And more terrible still, my loved ones
cannot escape him.   Is there nothing else?   Is death
the final master in the house, and is destiny con-
summated in him?

I go to another hill, and I lift mine eyes.   It is
the *hill called Olivet*.   And what is there?   The
Lord of Sinai is there.   The Lamb of Calvary is
there.   But He is there as the Lord of life.   On
Calvary I saw the Lord upon a Cross; on Olivet I
see Him clothed in deathless life.   He entered the
gates of death, He broke the power of death, He
came again the Conqueror of death.   On Sinai I
see the conquest of anarchy.   On Calvary I see the
conquest of sin.   On Olivet I see the conquest of
death.   Olivet blazes with the light of immortality.

And so this third hill is a wonderful minister in
the transformation of my life, and especially in the
transformation of its exit from this bourne of time
and space.   Olivet reveals to me that death is not a
terminus but a thoroughfare.   In Christ Jesus death
is not my master but my servant.   Olivet assures
me that the last word is not good-bye but good-
night, and it throws into my darkness the glorious
harbingers of dawn.   The music of the Gospel
sings to me of home.   Did not our Saviour say,
" If it were not so I would have told you "?   To
know the Lord of Olivet is to be immune from the
final dominion of death.   " Because I live ye shall
live also."   And, therefore, do men and women go
to Olivet, and in its spiritual inspiration they sing

such words as these—" For me to live is Christ, and to die is gain." And such words as these— " Whether we live we live unto the Lord, or whether we die we die unto the Lord: whether we live therefore or die we are the Lord's!" And such words as these—" So shall we be for ever with the Lord!" Only as Olivet is in our life can we use the words which are on Canon Wilberforce's honoured grave in the cloisters of the Abbey: " He lives, he wakes! 'Tis death is dead, not he!" Olivet is the mount of eternal morning.

XI

THE GRACE OF BENEFICENCE

"Therefore, as ye abound in everything, in faith, and utterance, and knowledge, and in all diligence, and in your love to us, see that ye abound in this grace also."
—2 CORINTHIANS viii. 7.

THERE is no letter of the Apostle Paul where his severity has more weight, and heat, and energy, than in his second letter to the Corinthians. Yet there is no letter where his tenderness is more sensitive, and more penetrating, and more exquisite. The severities of this letter are like the biting rigours of Alpine heights; its tendernesses are like the Alpine flowers. They are both part of the same moral landscape. They have their explanation in the same fundamental truth. In this letter there is stern indignation against anything and everything which would befoul the purity of Christian fellowship; on the other hand, there is a most affectionate craving that every believer in Christ might attain unto a spiritual completeness of character which shall be like some noble and symmetrical tree. Indeed, the Apostle watches the growth of these Corinthian disciples as a gardener tends the varied growths in his garden. The gardener prunes one thing, and he restrains another, while to others he gives stimulus and encouragement. In one place the gardener's ministry is like a nipping frost, in another place it is like a wooing sunbeam, but all the ministries are directed to the one purpose of leading the growing life into full-orbed maturity. And it is even so with the Apostle Paul and these believers in Corinth. He is watching their life with prayerful eagerness, and he is ceaselessly busy enticing grace after grace into visible strength. And here we find him cherishing yet another grace, and seeking by its development to still further enrich their character. " See that ye abound in this grace also."

What is this particular grace which is suggested in the phrase, " this grace also," and which he wishes to appear like bountiful clusters of grapes upon a vine? There is a sore famine in Jerusalem. There is a great dearth over the land. There is much suffering. The Christian believers in Jerusalem and elsewhere are sharing the pangs of want. Their necessity has gone out in a cry for help. The appeal has reached the Apostle Paul, and he brings the cry to Corinth. What kind of people are these disciples in Corinth to whom the apostle has to make this appeal? Their Christian character is marked by much moral and spiritual distinction. The Apostle mentions some of the excellencies in which they abound. They have " faith " which is a wealth of spiritual confidence and venture; it has a strength of trust in God which sends a man over rough roads on difficult journeys. And they have " utterance," power of expression, power to take truth and embody it in words, power to convert experience into testimony. And they have " knowledge, ' power of spiritual understanding, power to penetrate and interpret spiritual secrets. And they have " diligence," speed of ministry, readiness of apprehension, quickness of movement. And they have " love," which is just a central fund of goodness, a moral vitality, not soured by cynicism or chilled by meanness. Surely this is a very rich and bountiful character, and surely these are people to whom any appeal may be made with serenest confidence! And Paul makes his appeal for help for the needy folk in Jerusalem. We are in no doubt about the issue. We confidently anticipate the outpouring of a plentiful beneficence, a spontaneous overflow of sacrificial bounty.

And yet there is an uncertainty in the Apostle's tone. He is not quite sure of these people in Corinth. He reiterates his appeals. He repeats them with added emphasis. He recurs to it again and again, as if the stream of beneficence was not flowing with the fulness of healthy consecration. The appeal has run through chapter eight, and chapter nine, and chapter ten. He is greatly concerned that these fellow-believers should be distinguished by " this grace also." What can be the explanation of this seeming reluctance, this apparent restraint, in a character so full and radiant as theirs? I can only think of one explanation: they did not give much thought to the matter. It was not lack of heart, it was lack of attention. The position is by no means rare and unusual. People can be devotees of their religion without being very thoughtful. Men and women can be philosophers without being practical. They can be controversialists, and discuss a thousand things without being inwardly considerate. And there is nothing which so demands the pioneering work of sensitive attention, there is nothing to which thoughtfulness and chivalrous considerateness is so essential as the grace of beneficence and the spirit of sacrifice. There must be clear thinking if there is to be fine feeling, and there must be clear thinking if our generosity is to be as a cup that runneth over. It was true of the Corinthians, and it is equally true of us and of all men, that if we are to have " this grace also," the grace of a wise and plenteous beneficence, it will have to be made a matter of deliberate culture. It is not a thing which can be left to itself. And it is because the work of beneficence is so clamorously needful, and it is because the reaction of beneficence in life and character is so fertilizing, and it is because the absence of beneficence is so destructive and so unfriendly to the purpose of God that I am venturing to give it this prominence.

Now let us lay down three judgments in which I think we shall all be agreed. And the first judg-

ment is this: we are apt to be gravely deceived
about the extent of our beneficence, and we vastly
exaggerate the amount of money we give away.
The majority of people have no idea of the range of
their beneficence. It is not governed by any definite purpose. It is not a piloted enterprise. It does
not follow any pathway of appointed ministry. It
is not a crusade. It is a thing of chance and caprice. They do not know how much or how little
they give in the course of a year. But the bias of
their estimate is always on the side of generous
judgment. The people who do not know how
much they give always give less than they think
they do. Indeed some people's memories are of a
very perverted order; they lead them to estimate
their giving by the number of appeals which they
hear rather than by the number of responses which
they make to the appeals. And so it happens that
they esteem themselves to be generous when in reality they may be mean.

And the second judgment is this: there is a
strangely paralysing power about money, and it so
restricts the heart that the more we get the less we
are inclined to give. And this is surely what the
Lord meant when He spake of "the deceitfulness
of riches." Riches can make a man think that he is
growing bigger when all the time he is growing
less. He estimates his size by the inlet of income
and not by the outlet of beneficence. While the
inlet is expanding the outlet is contracting. But

the deception is frequently more deadly still. His growth in riches is often accompanied by a corresponding growth in fear. It is one of the pathetic ironies of life that men who are growing in wealth have an increasing fear of poverty. And the fear puts them into bonds and they are afraid to give of their treasure lest none should remain. I went to see a very wealthy man in New York to ask him to help an exceedingly noble cause. His fear immediately answered my appeal, and he spake as one who was on the verge of poverty: " I really cannot give any more!" The word was apparently sincere, and it was accompanied by a sort of sigh which confirmed its reality. " I really cannot give any more! What with one thing and another I do not know what we are coming to!" Fear seemed to haunt the man. It determined his thought and his speech and his services. A few weeks later he died, and his will was proved at over sixty millions! And I wonder, I wonder if at the end of the day he heard the messenger of the Lord saying unto him, " Thou fool, this night thy soul shall be required of thee, then whose shall these things be?"

And the third judgment is this: that conscience in the matter of giving is apt to become less sensitive as the appeals come from the necessities of the soul. Many a man will give generously in response to a cry of material hunger who is numb to the cry of spiritual hunger. Many men will give a large contribution to relieve the hungry children in Eastern Europe who feel no urgency in the cry of those who are spiritually hungry in Mongolia or Thibet. They would hasten to succor a fainting body but they are careless to the needs of a fainting heart.

Well, all these are personal chills in the service of beneficence. They are personal limitations, they are personal antagonisms, and they assault us all; and we are compelled to take a very strong and deliberate course if we are to overcome them and rise into possession of a soul which is nobly distinguished by "this grace also." How are we to meet these enemies of beneficence? What course can we follow to make beneficence a spontaneous issue in our life? First of all we must cultivate a sense of stewardship. We must cultivate the sense as assiduously as we have cultivated the sense of ownership and possession. If we want to know how to do it let us patiently give time to considering how we train and develop any other sense in our life, and then apply the teaching to this particular one. How do we cultivate a sense of reverence to the Most High? How do we cultivate a sense of loyalty to one's country? There are modes of doing these things, and if we follow the method of culture the sense and discernment will be formed. A sense of stewardship is the recognition of the ultimate Fountain of our life and strength; it is homage paid where homage is due. The Lord puts this homage very early in the prayer which He taught His disciples. The prayer first of all moves in mighty orbits:—" Our Father which art in heaven, Hallowed be Thy name, Thy Kingdom come, Thy will be done on earth as it is in heaven." And then from these vast movements it touches the commonplace of daily life. " Give us this day our daily bread." Our dependence is unveiled, and we are seen to be beneficiaries of the holy grace and love of God. It is not merely our bread but all our necessities which are brought near the altar and placed within the light of the great white Throne. " When thou hast eaten, and art full, then beware lest thou forget the Lord." In that way does the word of God reveal to us our dependence upon the Lord for all our possessions, and it is in the recognition of this dependence and obligation that we cultivate the sense of stewardship. All that we have is ours in trust; and we are to bow in homage before the Lord and say, " Not my will but Thine be done."

Another essential way of cultivating a really healthy spirit of beneficence is to exercise our conscience in the matter. Our beneficence is frequently determined by our emotions and not by our conscience. It is governed by the feeling of what we like to do and not by the imperative of what we ought to do. Government by the emotions is always a perilous and unstable kind of sovereignty. The emotions may be enfeebled, they may be dull and sluggish, and then the motive power becomes impotent. A religious life which is ruled by the feelings has a very faint initiative if the feelings are dried up. And so it is in the matter of beneficence. It is probably true of the majority of people that before their beneficence is active their feelings have to be excited and their emotions have to be fervid and boiling. And so the appeals are commonly directed to the feelings, and time after time speakers have to play upon the emotions in order to elicit support for such ministries as hospitals and Home and Foreign Missions. The consequence is, the giving is as uncertain and spasmodic as the movement of the emotions. We require a moral momentum which will create a bountiful beneficence even though our emotional moods are dry. We want to have even dry giving that is governed by the impelling action of the conscience. And so we must bring the appeals into the light of the conscience, and settle them by a sense of rectitude, even though we are not thrilled by appeals which are couched in eloquent and moving speech.

But we must do more than this. We must not only put homage and conscience into our beneficence, we must put method into it. We cannot fight the enemies of magnanimity and beneficence by thoughtless and spasmodic warfare. We must have a scheme of action. There must be method in the enterprise. We must have a plan of campaign. There must be some designed strategy if we are to overcome the deadly attacks of the grim

army of selfishness and meanness. And I am sure
that part of this sane method must be the assign-
ment of a certain minimum proportion of our income to ministries of beneficence. The minimum
must not be less than a tenth. Even the Pharisee
could boast of that attainment: " I give tithes of all
that I possess." It was no dull virtue when we
compare it with the general giving of the members
of the Church of Christ. If we all followed the
Pharisee's example, and gave a tenth of all that we
possessed, the appeals which call to our beneficence
would be met with overflowing wealth and sufficiency. But we must fix the minimum, not only for
the sake of the bounty, but for our own comfort
and peace. There is nothing more irritating than
to encounter appeals when we have no plan, and
when we do not know how much we are giving, or
how much we have given. There is a great sense
of power, and satisfaction, and peace when we
know just where we are, and what we are doing,
and what we are able to do. The method orders
our beneficence, and gives a feeling of readiness,
and we are partly on the way with our response
even before the appeal is made.

But I would advise young people who adopt the
method of minimum proportion not to drivel their
tenth away in small and insignificant contributions.
Let them go in sometimes for the giving of large
sums. If you have ten pounds a year to give away,
have the satisfaction now and again of giving a

five-pound note to something. If you do it you will know the reason of the counsel. It seems a big sum, and it challenges your powers, and there is a bracing influence in the endeavour. The subsequent experience will give you the needful justification. It is like a fine drive at golf; if it is a good send off and the lesser strokes will come in its train. And if you find, as the year goes by, that the tenth is exhausted, you may take a dash past your minimum and break all your records. You will do it just to prove that you are not the victim of your own minimum. It will be like a plunge into deep cold water and you will emerge with a very healthy glow, not the fever of silly pride but the satisfaction of healthy manhood. You will rejoice in the health of God's countenance for you are a willing co-operator with the Lord. It is surely well to train our young children in these methodical ways. If they begin early and are taught to regard their little possessions in homage, and with conscience, and with method, the fine habit will become fine instinct from the very beginning of their days.

I confess I am very much concerned about this grace and virtue of beneficence in the Christian life and character. The generosity of our people during the war was manifold and amazing. Every appeal was met with fervour, and our folk were strengthened by the energies of their own beneficence. But beneficence which flows freely in days of conflict may dry up again in the quieter days of peace. The necessity may seem to be over and the fountain goes to sleep. That is one of our dangers. And the other equally imminent danger is this: we are surely living in a day of extravagance. There are signs of wasteful and even prodigal squandering on every side. We have the example of Governments which are not taking the lead in wise economy. We have Governments steadily and obstinately proposing that we spend millions in decking up militarism in glaring and alluring attire. This is the kind of evil leadership which acts contagiously upon the whole country. Think of what is being spent in pleasure. Look at the crowded theatres and the cinemas with their long waiting queues. I do not object to these things, and I appreciate the reasonable reaction after all the strain and the fear and terror of the war. But it is unhealthy when we spend a large proportion of our income on amusement and have no reserves to meet the demands of noble necessity. Millions of professedly Christian people give more money to see one performance in a cinema than they give to the cause of God's kingdom in a whole year. I do not attribute this lack of beneficence to meanness, or to a stinginess which locks up its resources; it is explained by want of thoughtfulness, and by lack of method, and conscience, and piloted devotion.

The constraints which ought to move us are great and manifold. There are the needs them-

selves. Let us direct our thoughts and our imagination to play about the realms of necessity. Let
us make the dead facts live by the breath of our
own life. Let us vitalize them with living thought
so that far-away necessities come and stand and
breathe at our door.

And then let us walk with Jesus Christ. Let us
talk with Him. Let us ask for His counsel. Let
us hear what He has to say about things. Let us
consult Him about this, and that, and the other,
and our hearts will burn within us as He talks with
us by the way. His own example will be our abiding constraint. " Ye know the grace of our Lord
Jesus Christ, that though He was rich, yet for our
sakes He became poor, that ye through His poverty
might be rich." When we follow the young Prince
of Glory from His Throne to His Cross the springs
of sacrifice are unsealed in our own hearts, we have
the fellowship of His sufferings, and in the realm
of beneficence we become ready and cheerful givers.

XII

THE SPIRITUAL GLOW

"Be fervent in spirit."—ROMANS xii. 11.
"Maintain the spiritual glow" (Dr. Moffatt's Translation).

I WANT to consider the defensive power of a noble enthusiasm. What do I mean by an enthusiasm? I mean an intense and generous passion for some supreme interest, so passionate that it dominates the life. And what do I mean by the defensive powers of such an enthusiasm? I mean that such a passion gathers all the forces of life into its own swift goings, so that nothing is left to loiter, nothing is left to trail along in aimless vagrancy. Every power is caught in the commanding suction of a great enthusiasm; it is not trapped by any insidious enticement which may be lurking by the way. A noble enthusiasm is defensive because it makes life whole and wholesome. This kind of fire tends to keep everything clean.

Turn where you please you may watch the protective influence of a great enthusiasm. Take a young fellow who goes to one of our national Universities. What does he find? He finds pernicious influences of many kinds. There are germs of enervation which would reduce him to mental lassitude. There are soft enticements which would lull him into moral laxity. But give him a passion for learning, and all these small invaders are burnt up in the fervent heat. A bewitching pleasure, a luring indolence, a seductive mischief—his enthusiasm destroys them as in a consuming fire. The assailments shrivel like moths in a flame. His passion is his defence.

So it is with the reign of any predominant enthusiasm. It has protective ministry. Give a working man a passion for gardening and put him into an allotment, and what defensive forces his enthusiasm throws round about his leisure hours! All the meaner enticements lose their power. They never reach his central consciousness. Indeed, there is no consciousness to spare. His enthusiasm commands all his forces, and the baser things call to him in vain. His fire is his defence.

It is even so with the passionate championship of some great ideal. Emerson's counsel has now become a familiar phrase: " Hitch your wagon to a star! " It is the wedding of idealism to very mundane tasks. It is Emerson's way of saying that even the drawing of a cart along a muddy road can be associated with lofty and shining ideals. Wagons can be drawn by starry steeds. Humdrum tasks can be harnessed to heavenly coursers. There can be a noble passion in common toil. Yes, and when we do hitch our wagon to a star, we may be perfectly sure that, whatever the star may do for the wagon, it will irradiate the wagoner and protect him by the ministry of sacred flame. When he arrives with his wagon at the end of the road, be the wagon empty or full, he himself will be as clean as a priest of the Lord; nay, he is a priest of the Lord, clothed in linen pure and white, ministering at the altar of labour, on which there burns the fire divine. His fiery passion is his defence.

But, when enthusiasm begins to cool, our defensive energy begins to wane. As the fire dies out the enemy comes in. Just as soon as radiation ceases invasion begins. Mean things appear, and they appear in aggressive pride. It is as when the temperature of the blood is reduced. Waiting plague and lurking disease find entry and foothold and they begin to thrive in the defenceless roads of the flesh. Admiral Peary has told us, in his account of the discovery of the North Pole, that it was in the dreary, weary Arctic winter, when enthusiasm waned, that the hidden weaknesses of his men appeared. It was then that the spirit of irritation and dissension would breathe disturbing air upon the fellowship. As the fires died low quarrelsomeness stole in. The moral defences departed with the glow. And so it is in every relationship of life. When noble fires are burning our estates are secure. When the noble fires smoulder our estates are invaded, and mean and baser things possess our spiritual world.

And so, right in the midst of all this, there

comes this word of the Apostle Paul, " Be fervent
in spirit." Keep your fires burning! Maintain a
spiritual glow! This urgent counsel was given to a
little company of disciples who were living their
consecrated life in the city of Rome. Think of
their environment. They breathed a moral atmosphere full of deadly germs. They were surrounded
by the seductive, destructive lure of Mammon.
They felt the ceaseless power of the down-dragging
magnetism of worldly gravity. They were beset
by evil incitements and suggestions and antagonisms. They lived and moved where the majesty of
evil had its throne and sovereignty.

And the Apostle Paul tells them that nothing but
a passionate religion will endow them with needful
resistance. Tepid devotion will afford no defences.
Luke-warmness will be the friend of contagion.
Nothing but exuberant and overflowing health will
afford protection from the moral plague. If the
fires go out Rome will come in. So be fervent in
spirit! Maintain the spiritual glow! Keep the
home fires burning! Let them burn like the live
coal which glows upon the altar of God.

Now I will contend that there is no other counsel
of the Apostle which is more urgent and timely for
our own day. Now, as then, our spiritual enthusi-
asms are our moral defences. If our devotion to
Christ burns with an intense fervour, if it burns as
with a core of glowing heat, the mean and deadly
things which beset us will be consumed as in a fiery

furnace. God still purifies Jerusalem, and He keeps her pure by the spirit of burning.

Let us turn the light of the Apostle's counsel upon the individual life and let us see what guidance it gives us in the personal welfare of the soul. When our devotion to Christ maintains a spiritual glow everything in our life shares the gracious influence of the quickening heat. Every power experiences the stirring of the heavenly warmth. Life is energized from the central fire, and every noble faculty begins to disclose its purposed strength and glory. It is like it is in a green-house, the basal heat quickens every plant to increase its stature and to clothe itself in floral beauty. Or better still, it is like a garden where every unsprung seed thrills to the common touch of the spring-tide sun. So when there is a spiritual glow in life everything begins to be fulfilled; we are becoming complete in the Lord, who rises upon us with healing in His wings.

And as such a fire-possessed life is whole and wholesome so is it also secure. Its fire is its defence. When night falls upon the explorer in African jungle he seeks for a clearing, and he lights a fire, and the cheery flame is his protection against the prowling beast. Our picnic fire puts the mosquito to flight. And so it is with our spiritual fire, it keeps the beast at bay, and it resists the hornet that carries the plague. Our fire is our defence. "He was clad with zeal as with a cloak," and when a man is wearing that cloak of fire he is encased in armour of invincible security.

But if our fires abate, if our passion cools, if our devotion to Christ Jesus loses its fervour, the issues run to gloomy destiny. Every noble faculty of life feels the withdrawal of the central heat. Our graded powers are like a regiment which has lost its *esprit de corps*, and every sacred gift becomes a weakling in the ranks. Aye, but more than this, the lessening of the fires means the loss of our defences. When the fire smoulders the poison-laden hornet is again on the wing. When the fire in the forest dies down, the wild beast always draws near. How urgent then is the Apostolic counsel: "Maintain your spiritual glow!" Keep the heart fires burning! And thou shalt not be afraid of the pestilence that walketh in darkness, nor of the destruction that wasteth at noonday.

Now turn the light of the Apostle's counsel to social fellowship, and let it fall upon the corporate life of the Church. When there is a spiritual glow in the Church mean things are consumed like dirt in a furnace. The spiritual radiations of the Church ensure its moral security. But let the Church lose her spiritual glow and all manner of un-Christly things swarm across her desecrated floors. We have a glaring example of all this in the state of the Church at Corinth as it is revealed to us by the Apostle Paul. The fires in the Church had burned low, they had burnt down almost to grey ashes amid the deadly besetments of Corinth, and one has only to read the Apostle's letter to the Corinthians to find out what manner of unclean things crowded her sacred courts. The wild beast entered the holy place in the shape of unnameable vices. Sordid moods found a prolific resource. Petty partisanship became common. Peddling questionings began to abound. There was an emphasis of things external, there was an exaltation of ritual and traditions. There was bickering, and quarrelling, and gossip. The fires in the Church died down, and the world streamed in.

I think there is an equally startling revelation of the smallness which invades a lukewarm Church in the example of the Church at Jerusalem. The Church in Jerusalem had no missionary enthusiasm because it had lost its spiritual glow. It had no flaming evangel because it had lost its fire. It had no speeding Seraphim because its altars were cold. When the great missionary Apostle returned from the last and greatest of his missionary tours he reported his work to the Church in Jerusalem. And what happened? Paul had kindled a line of holy fires through Asia Minor. Sacred beacons were blazing in Macedonia and lower Greece. Isles of the sea had become luminous with the light of life. He had incurred perils innumerable. He had been ceaselessly pursued by the cruel hounds of persecution. He had been flung into prison. He had been scourged. He carried the scars of travail. He bore the marks of the Lord Jesus. And he was now old and broken, but his quenchless fire was burning, and he told his glowing story to the Apostles and Church at Jerusalem. " He declared particularly what God had wrought among the Gentiles by his ministry." And what did they say about it? In what kind of holy rapture did they express their glowing praise? " Thou knowest, brother, how many thousands of Jews there are which believe, and they are all zealous of the law." Yes, and what next? Can you think what is coming? They urged him to take a purifying vow and to shave his head! Can you imagine that if that Church had been glowing with a passion of devotional love to the Lord, such a peddling bit of Jewish ritual would have been forced into a season of spiritual wonder and exuberance? I know the great Apostle did it: yes, I know he did it; but I think I also know that in doing it he became obedient unto death, even the death of the Cross.

I repeat that when the Church of Christ loses its spiritual glow ritual becomes more than miracles of grace, and hierarchical orders and ministries obscure the blazing wonders of the Holy Ghost. It is as though the venerable General Booth had returned from one of his glorious evangelistic journeys in which thousands of souls had opened their windows to the saving light of God's most marvellous dawn, and he had told the story of grace to some episcopal convocation, and had been met by

the response: " Brother, there are many thousands
of believers who are zealous of the ecclesiastical
law.   Do this, therefore, that we say to thee: receive ordination to the ministry by the laying on of
episcopal hands."   To which, I think, the old warrior would have replied: " I live, yet not I, Christ
liveth in me, and the life which I now live in the
flesh, I live by the faith of the Son of God, who
loved me and gave Himself for me."   " For me
to live is Christ! "

But we need not go to ancient Corinth or Jerusalem to learn that when the great glow departs from
the Church smaller things come in.   Do you think
there would ever have been a Kikuyu controversy
if there had been a glowing, passionate devotion to
Christ?   Do you think we should be so tremblingly
discussing interchange of pulpits if we were aflame
with love for our Lord?   Do you think we should
be painfully concerned with the form and colour of
ritualistic raiment if we were clad with zeal as with
a cloak?   These things stand high when fires burn
low.   When the spiritual glow goes out of the
Church the organism is supplanted by the organiza-
tion, the vital is changed for the institutional, the
Christly becomes the Churchly, and ecclesiastical
orders have more emphasis than the divine grace.

It is needful for us to remember, in our own ecclesiastical realm, and in the face of modern striv-
ings, that we must have glow before we can gain
union.   I have sometimes felt that we were like

foolish blacksmiths who were seeking to weld luke-warm bars of iron into a single piece. We were ecclesiastical blacksmiths trying to weld luke-warm Churches into vital Communion. I do not think it is blacksmith's work at all. The Scriptures say nothing about welding sundered things into vital fellowship, but they do speak about separated things flowing together into union. What a difference there is between welding things and the same things flowing together! But before things can flow together they must have become molten. We must have molten affections, fluid sympathies; we must have genialities and fraternities flowing like molten streams from a central fire. And therefore does the Apostle urge us to maintain a spiritual glow. Let the Church of Christ do this, and in the blazing devotion we shall flow together as kindred streams of heavenly flame.

Now, at the end of all this, may I not suggest, as an additional vista of meditation, that in international life peoples become one only in the uniting energies of noble fire? There is something about the binding power of a passionate crusade which resists every poisonous incitement and every perilous lure. These things flee before a generous enthusiasm as snakes and vipers flee before a prairie fire. We have seen the uniting power of a commanding passion in the fiery travail of the Great War. I know not how it may have been in diplomatic circles; the tortuous ways of diplomacy sometimes seem to be the last roads to be reached by the heat of a noble passion. But as for the allied peoples, those who flamed in the sacred charge, they surely become one in the fire of common duty, common danger, common hope, and common sacrifice. Old estrangements were knit together in vital fellowship. Old perversities were consumed like autumn leaves in a gardener's fire. We trusted where we had suspected, we cheered where we had frowned, we admired where we had criticized. We flowed together.

And all this was especially true in the relation of the British and American peoples. Old prejudices melted away like icebergs in tropical seas. Antipathies which were the creation of a hundred years changed into friendship. Stony moods which were the petrifactions of generations softened into the kindly amenities of kindred flesh and blood. We found each other, and we saw each other, in the revealing fires of a vast enthusiasm, and all the meaner things perished like stubble in the flame. Are we maintaining the glow? I confess that to me the old evil things seem to be creeping back again. Are the noble fires smouldering? I think I see the critical spirit contending with the fraternal. I think I see good-will hardening here and there into the old suspicion. I think I see the peril of intimate comradeship drawing apart again into the cold aloofness of ancient prejudice. What I call the hair-trigger mood, the touch-and-fire mood, is asserting itself again. On the one side there is American touchiness, susceptible as the eye-ball; on the other side there are signs of British superciliousness and pride. On the one hand we hear suggestions that Jonathan has harked back to his dollars again. On the other hand we have suggestions that John Bull has reverted to his old game of double dealing and his successful practice of up-the-sleeve diplomacy. All of which means that the old stinging hornets are buzzing in the air again. It means that the old beasts are beginning to " home " again on the international fields.

Now, what is to save us? Nothing but the spiritual glow. We can repel and destroy these emerging evils by feeding the fires of a large and noble enthusiasm. Everybody can help in making the fire. Everybody can bring fuel to the holy flame. We can strengthen it with knowledge, we can feed it with thought, we can quicken it with expression, we can deepen it with prayer. We can live and labour for the passion of fraternity, the enthusiasm of humanity, the glow of Christ, the fire of God.

Our resource, in all our imminent problems, and in all the difficulties which confront us, is to be found in the maintenance of the spiritual glow. I see no hope for the world except in common and enthusiastic devotion to our Lord Jesus Christ. And by devotion to Christ I mean something loftier than ecclesiastical passion, and something far nobler than denominational pride. I mean that vital, personal, quickening relationship to the Saviour which fills the mind and heart with generous and cleansing passion. I mean the spiritual devotion which makes a life conspicuous for magnanimity, chivalry, fraternity, humanity. That fire of God can cleanse the world!

> Come Holy Spirit, Heavenly dove,
>   With all Thy quickening powers
> Kindle a flame of sacred love
>   On these cold hearts of ours.

XIII

TO WHOM SHALL WE GO?

"From that time many of His disciples went back, and walked no more with Him. Then said Jesus unto the twelve, Will ye also go away? Then Simon Peter answered Him, Lord, to whom shall we go? thou hast the words of eternal life."—JOHN vi. 66-68.

IN this incident the Lord is hearing the early murmurings of final rejection. The chilling airs of a darkening twilight are already on the road. Deep shadows are falling about Him. He has begun to assert His own claims more imperatively, and He is laying heavier demands upon the faith of men and upon their loyalty and obedience. Discipleship had been regarded as a smooth and flowery road, leading to earthly power and glory, a noble highway terminating in a throne. But now the Master is speaking mysterious words about drinking His blood. Stern antagonisms begin to appear on the way. The terrific figure of death is seen approaching, and all the coveted flowers are beginning to wither, and every bird is losing its song. The disciples had imagined they were marching onward to worldly crowns and dominions; and now their entire horizon is filled with a looming and threatening cross, the symbol of final

tragedy and confusion. " And many of His disciples went back, and walked no more with Him."
There is something very cold about the desertion,
and the gathering sense of desolation is deepened
when the Master turns to those who are left
and says, " Will ye also go away?" And Simon
Peter, with a swift impulsiveness which often
tripped him into disaster, but which quite as
often led him into realms of truth and rich experience, answered Him, saying, " Lord, to whom
shall we go? Thou hast the words of eternal
life."

Well now, who is this Peter who thus proclaims
the Lord Jesus as the only fountain of spiritual
satisfaction? Is he a man of any distinction? Or
is he a man of shallow being, whose small capacities
are easily filled? We are sometimes inclined to
speak of the disciples as though they were just
twelve average men, whose gifts were about on a
par with any other twelve men whom we might
meet in the street. But I am not so sure about
that. I am not inclined to regard a fisherman as a
type of the average man. There is something about
a real fisherman which appeals to me as very distinguished. His very calling is the minister of
enlargement; its perils, its vastness, the sweep of
the encompassing heavens, the far-spreading ocean-
wastes reaching to dim horizons; the height, and
depth, and breadth; the silences, the broodings, the
mysterious presences, the sense of the Infinite!

No, I cannot regard the fisherman's life as a common life, nor can I look upon the fisherman as an average man; and I think it is deeply significant that fishermen have given us so large a part of the New Testament. They have given us the epistle of James, the epistle of Peter, the epistles of John, the Book of Revelation, and the richest treasure of them all, the Gospel by John. And I love to cherish the thought that perhaps the immensities of their daily life were no mean part of the ministry which expanded their beings to receive the immensities of revelation, the unfolding of the wonderful gospel of redeeming grace.

Here, then, is one of these fishermen who has just answered the pathetic question of our Lord, "Will ye also go away?" by the counter-question "To whom shall we go?" "Where is there another teacher who can give to us what Thou dost give? If we leave Thee we leave everything! Thou hast the words of eternal life." Well, what did Jesus Christ do for Simon Peter? We have his life before us; it is recorded in the Word. His letters have been preserved; they are bound up in the Word. What, then, did Jesus Christ do for this man which He could have found nowhere else? And I ask the question on the assurance that what Christ Jesus did for Simon Peter He can do for everybody, and that all lives, which may be externally very different from Simon Peter's, can be filled with a kindred satisfaction. What, then, did

Jesus do for Peter? Turn to Peter's life and letters.

First of all, *Jesus Christ gave Simon Peter a new God.* When you change a man's conception of God it is as though his God had become new. In these realms a new revelation is a new creation. In what way can we realize the newness of Peter's God? It is sometimes an exceedingly instructive experience, even in common literature, to pass quickly from one book to another, in the attempt to realize the difference in their atmospheres. Take a biography down from your shelves, or a book of letters, and read just enough pages to feel the climate. And then take down another, and stay long enough in the second to get the feeling of the general weather and temperature; and you will find the contrast in the two atmospheres to be most instructive. For instance, take the life of Tennyson, and read almost any chapter you please, and then pass swiftly into the life of Thomas Carlyle, and read almost any chapter you please; and the almost violent change in the climate will tell you much about the constitution of their lives. Or read a chapter in the life of Tolstoy, and then, almost with a leap, pass into the life of Napoleon, and you will find that it is not only the external events which are in such vivid contrast, but the very air, the temperature, the skyey influences, the mystic breath. Read twenty pages of the life of Cecil Rhodes, and then twenty pages of the life of Emerson, and you will find yourself in two absolutely different worlds with a different heaven and a different earth.

And then, take the book of Amos, and move about in that book for an hour, looking up, and down, and around, and especially watching and brooding upon the God revealed in that book. And then, by a swift transition, pass to a letter of Peter's, and look upon his God as revealed to him in Jesus Christ our Lord. Do the same with the book of Hosea, that tender little revelation, which is as sweet in many places as rich meadows that are drenched with dew. Do it with Jeremiah. Then turn again to Peter. I am suggesting that you make these little journeys in order that you may feel the contrast in the two climates and in the two skies. Take one of the imprecatory Psalms, and look at its God, and then bathe your eyes in a chapter of Peter, and look out upon his God; and you will feel as though you have passed from a blast-furnace, shooting forth its fires by night, to the wooing glory of a serene and radiant dawn. Or read a chapter or two in the mysterious and complicated symbolism of Ezekiel, and then turn your perplexed and wearied eyes to a paragraph or two in Peter, and you will feel as though you had turned from some very trying glare to the cooling presence of green pastures, and to gracious simplicities of love which feed the soul with the bread of life.

I am suggesting to you that Simon Peter had

hitherto been living in the climate of the Old Testament, under the Old Testament sky, and in the Old Testament world. But when Jesus came, Simon Peter found a new mental and spiritual climate, for he found a new heaven and a new earth in the new revelation of God. It was a tremendous day for Simon Peter when he heard Christ Jesus say, " He that hath seen Me hath seen the Father." From that day, " old things were passed away; behold all things became new!" . . . "Lord, to whom shall we go?" Thou hast the word of revelation. " Thou hast the words of eternal life."

What else did Jesus Christ give to Simon Peter? *Jesus Christ gave to Simon Peter a new relationship to God.* The new God revealed in Christ Jesus was not afar off, like some dazzling snow-white mountain which could never be climbed. The new revelation was not some uplifted and resplendent glory which mocked him by its very remoteness. The Christ who made the revelation of God to Simon Peter also established a new relation between Simon Peter and God. Before Jesus came Peter felt himself to be only a connection of God; now he knew himself to be a relation. You can feel the difference in the two words which I am using in the attempt to express it. A connection is legal, formal, external, cold. A relation is spiritual, inward, vital. A doll's arm is connected with a doll's body; but my arm is related to my body by vital processes of blood, and by even more mystic

currencies which cannot be expressed. Simon
Peter was once connected with God; in Christ
Jesus he has found a vital relation. Once he was
far off; now he is nigh. Once he was alienated;
now he is reconciled. Once he was in bonds in a
far country; now he is redeemed from bondage and
finds himself at home. Once he was a servant;
now he is a son. Now he is of the blood-royal, of
heaven's best blood, with titles manifold. If you
read his letters you will again and again hear the
wedding bells ringing announcing the marriage of
his soul with the Lord. The revelation of God has
issued in a new relation, and the grace of the Lord
Jesus has done it! . . . "Will ye also go away?"
"Lord, to whom shall we go? Thou hast the word
of reconciliation. Thou hast the words of eternal
life."

And there are many other things which Jesus did
for Simon Peter, all of which spring from the new
revelation of the Father, and from the new relationship to the Father begotten in His Son. For
one thing, *Jesus had given Peter a new conception
of man.* It will be altogether worth your while to
take these letters of Simon Peter, and just pick out
the separate lineaments of his ideal man, and then
so compose them that you can gaze upon the face
of the ideal character. It can be done, just as you
might compose Plato's ideal man from Plato's
works, or Byron's ideal man, or Thomas Carlyle's.
You can take Peter's letters, and bit by bit you can

construct his man in Christ Jesus, until the man shines before you, a radiant personality. The Lord Jesus gave Peter a new conception of man, and Peter's new ideal was in the likeness and glory of the Nazarene.

And with all these wonderful gifts *Jesus Christ also gave to Peter an all-sufficient moral dynamic.* For what are revelations worth without inspirations? And what is the worth of ideals if they are accompanied by no dynamics? And what is the good of high callings if we have no wings? If the veil is lifted upon the ideal man, and we gaze upon him in all the alluring glory of his holiness, what is its value unless the Revealer can impart to us some mystic energy which can nourish virtue and sap the roots of vice? The moral ideal is only welcome as it is accompanied by moral motive and moral constraint. And if you will read the life and letters of Simon Peter you will find plenty of evidence that this holy moral energy was poured into this man's being in such gracious abundance that weakness became strength, and timidity was changed into courage, and inconstancy, which had once trembled at the threatenings of a maid, was transformed into a fidelity which greeted martyrdom with a song, and went forth to death as lightly as a bride trips forth to meet her bridegroom. And Jesus did it! Jesus did it!

And added to all other gifts the Lord Jesus gave to Simon Peter *the glorious hope of immortality.*

You cannot read this man's letters without finding the hope of immortality throwing its interpreting beams on every page. You have scarcely begun to read the first letter before you come upon this illumining mass of glory: " Blessed be the God and Father of our Lord Jesus Christ, which according to His abundant mercy hath begotten us again unto a lively hope by the resurrection of Jesus Christ from the dead, to an inheritance incorruptible, and undefiled, and that fadeth not away, reserved in heaven for you." And the light of that great hope sends its radiance over everything, until even suffering itself is tipped with gold, and is lit with the glory of our eternal home. And Jesus did it!

I have only just begun to mention the things which Simon Peter found in Christ, and yet what glory has already been revealed! Christ Jesus gave Simon Peter a new God; He gave him a new relationship to God; He gave him a new conception of man, and a new ideal of the riches of human fellowship; He gave him an altogether adequate moral dynamic; and over all the ups and downs of Simon Peter's changing road the Saviour flung the light of eternal hope.

And now, what shall *we* do with this Jesus? Shall we leave Him? Where then shall we go? If we throw Jesus over, where shall we direct our steps? When our life is all in pieces, when we are confused and broken, where shall we turn? When our consciences are disquieted, when our wills are maimed, when evil habits have fastened invincible chains upon our souls, at whose door shall we knock for relief? When the floods of sorrow are out, and we are well-nigh overwhelmed, to whom shall we cry for deliverance? When the light of our eyes has gone out, and when desire and purpose have left us altogether, where shall we look for the re-kindling of our smouldering lamps and fires? If not to Jesus, then to whom shall we go?

What are the alternatives? There are some classic sentences in John Bunyan's " Pilgrim's Progress " which I should like to read to you:

I saw a man clothed with rags, standing in a certain place, with his face from his own house, and a book in his hand, and a great burden upon his back. . . . And he broke out into a lamentable cry saying, What shall I do? . . . And I saw in my dream that the highway up which Christian was to go was fenced on either side with a wall, and that wall was called Salvation. Up this way, therefore, did burdened Christian run, but not without great difficulty because of the load on his back. He ran thus till he came to a place somewhat ascending; and upon that place stood a Cross, and a little below, in the bottom, a Sepulchre. So I saw in my dream, that just as Christian came up with the Cross his burden loosed from off his shoulders, and fell from off his back, and began to tumble, and so continued to do, till it came to the mouth of the Sepulchre, where it fell in and I saw it no more.

That is what John Bunyan said Jesus did for his pilgrim. But suppose that in our day we desert the Lord Jesus, and forsake His Cross! Suppose we turn our backs upon all the wonderful deliverance begotten of our Saviour's life and love and passion, where shall we go? How would you re-write Bunyan's famous passage, and bring it up to date?

How would this do? " I saw a man clothed with rags, with a great burden upon his back. . . . Up this way did the pilgrim run, but not without difficulty, because of the load upon his back. So I saw in my dream that just when the pilgrim came up to *the hypnotist*." Is this the alternative? And what is going to happen there? What is this modern saviour going to do for a man whose past is a by-word, whose present is a humiliation, and whose future is black with despair? Is this the alternative to our Lord?

Or shall we amend the passage in this way? " I saw a man clothed in rags, and with a great burden upon his back. And he broke out with a loud lamentation, crying, ' What shall I do? ' Up this way did the pilgrim run. So I saw in my dream that just when the pilgrim came up to the *secularist . . .!* " And what will happen there? What has this modern substitute for Jesus to say to us? What is the secularist's counsel? This is his treatment! " Pack thy life," he says, " within the confines of the immediate day. Shut down all obstinate questionings. Close thy windows. Draw the shades. Silence these blank misgivings of a creature moving about in worlds not realized. Limit thy regard to the present hour. Take things as they come. Deal only with human interests, and

human relations.   Deal with the actual practical
things of daily life.   Shut out the unseen.   Forget
God!   Ignore eternity!" . . . So I saw in my
dream that the pilgrim, with the burden still upon
his back, turned from the secularists to carry out
his counsel.   And with what result:

> Just when we are safest, there's a sunset touch,
> A fancy from a flower-bell—someone's death,
> And that's enough for fifty hopes and fears,
> As old and new at once as nature's self,
> To rap and knock and enter in our soul,
> Take hands and dance there a fantastic ring,
> Round the ancient idol, on his base again,—
> The grand Perhaps! We look on helplessly.
> There the old misgivings, crooked questions are.

Is the secularist the alternative to our Lord.   Or,
finally, shall we amend Bunyan's classic in this
way?   "I saw a man, clothed with rags, with a
great burden upon his back.   Up this way did the
pilgrim run, but not without great difficulty because
of the load on his back.   So I saw in my dream that
just as the pilgrim came up to *the agnostic* . . .*!"*
Is that the alternative?   What has he to say to the
pilgrim's quest and questionings?   Nothing.   Let
me hear the pilgrim lay his pathetic need before
him.   " Sir, when my mind is haunted with the fear
of God, and my soul is disquieted with me, hast
thou any anodynes or balms?" . . . No answer.
" Sir, when my days are broken with the sense of
guilt and shame, and when my sin pursues me
like a shadow, dost thou know any welcome

hostel where a weary captive can find release?"
. . . No answer. "Sir, when the sorrows of life
pound all my little garden into a soddened mass
and marsh, hast thou any hiding place from the
storm?" . . . No answer. "Sir, when the part-
ner of my heart, light of my light, life of my life,
leaves me and passes into the night, and I lay the
body in the cold ground, and my hungry soul looks
forward to the morning, hast thou any good news,
any light of hope, any softening gleam to throw
upon my cross and care?" . . . No answer. . . .
Silence!

What then? Good-bye hypnotist, secularist,
agnostic, atheist! Good-bye, I am going home to
Christ. When I need Him most He is most unto
me. He fills the noontide with a fuller light, and
He opens a great and hospitable shelter in the midnight and the storm. Jesus Christ is "a hiding
place from the wind, a covert from the tempest, as
rivers of water in a dry place, and as the shadow
of a great rock in a weary land."

"Will ye also go away?" Lord, to whom shall
we go?

> I've tried the broken cisterns, Lord,
>   But ah! the waters failed;
> E'en as I stooped to drink they fled,
>   And mocked me as I wailed.
> Now none but Christ can satisfy,
>   None other name for me.
> There's life, and peace, and lasting joy,
>   Lord Jesus, found in Thee.

XIV

REALITY AND MYSTERY

"The wind bloweth where it listeth, and thou hearest the sound thereof, but canst not tell whence it cometh and whither it goeth: so is everyone that is born of the Spirit."—JOHN iii. 8.

LET us try to get the feeling of the happenings on this eventful night. It is the month of April. The land is beginning to be fragrant with the treasures of the Spring. And there is a man of the Pharisees named Nicodemus, a member of the acknowledged spiritual aristocracy of the Jewish people. He had been moved by the words and deeds of one Jesus, a Nazarene. Again and again he had sought more intimate knowledge of this mysterious Being, and he had thereby incurred the contempt of his fellow believers. He was stirred with disquietude. Some inner chord in his spirit began to vibrate like an Æolian harp when touched by the fingers of the wind. The little he knew made him eager to know more. He would dearly like the privilege of personal communion. But the menace of his sect was heavy and immediate. He was timid. He was not ready for courageous venture. Truth was luring him, but he was not yet a fearless crusader in her quest. He would follow her under the cloak of the night.

So when the darkness had fallen he left this home and went through the quiet streets. He went down the roadway outside the city gate and crossed over the brook Kedron. He climbed the slope of the Mount of Olives to the camp of the Galileans, where Jesus lived. He sought out the tent of the Nazarene, and the two men drew apart in the moonlight and walked away among the olive trees. Their conversation probably lasted all through the night, and yet the record which is given to us is less than three hundred words. What we are told is like the stakes which are erected across moorland tracks to indicate the way, and we can discern the road of their intercourse. Their conversation wound through mystery after mystery. And again and again Nicodemus broke into the words of the Master with the wistful plea, " How can these things be? " " How? " " How? " " How? " Again and again his intellect faltered and the mystery of things plunged him into bewilderment. And toward morning a wind breathed through the olive trees and set all the leaves a-whispering. And the Lord caught hold of it and made it the messenger of the truth. " The wind bloweth where it listeth; thou hearest the sound thereof, but canst not tell whence it cometh and whither it goeth." It is reality though it is a mystery. Its presence and movement are certain although its secrets are undisclosed. The wind is a minister of vitality even though its origin and its destiny can never be traced. It impresses itself upon us with firm assurance, yet it brings no luminous satisfaction to the intellect. " The wind thou hearest is a reality trailing clouds of mystery." " Thou canst not tell whence it cometh and whither it goeth." Nicodemus felt the breathings of the morning air although he had no knowledge of its birthplace or its grave.

So it is with the things of the Spirit. The great Teacher told this disquieted Pharisee that there are momentous happenings in the world of the Spirit, and their reality is not in the least degree impaired by the absence of a rational explanation. We can be sure of the wind even though we cannot explain it. We can be sure of spiritual realities even though reason limp and loiter on the road. In a word, we can have experience long before we have explanation. We can have spiritual reality before intellectual clarity. We can have life before light. We can be sure of the wind even when reason has not put its mysteries into bonds.

Now this is not a disparagement of the intellect. We do not disparage things by placing them in their appointed rank and order. We do not disparage the fruit of a tree when we place it in the autumn-time rather than in the spring. I do not disparage the alphabet when I say that a child can talk long before he knows that the alphabet exists. It is just a matter of grade, and order and succession. And when it is said that in the realm of the Spirit we can have happenings which are impressive before they are expressive, that life can have communion with realities before intellect has made her survey and begun to offer explanations, we are only proclaiming the divine order, and we are saying that the loitering intellect does not impoverish my assurance because of its delay.

Reality and mystery! The two are wedded together continually. It is even so with love. Love is a tremendous reality of which the reason itself can offer no explanation. And when reason makes a venturesome attempt to explain it the result is always grotesque. Have you ever read what professes to be an intellectual explanation of love? If you have the opportunity, read the philosophic analysis of love which Professor Bain gives in his book on the emotions; or take any book of moral philosophy, and wander down its highroads of detailed analysis of human affection, and then return to your own love of your fiancée, or of your wife, or of your child. And it is like returning from some dull herbarium, where everything is dry and withered, to the wild flowers of nature and to the wandering perfumes of the honeyed woods. Love itself is a glorious reality. But intellect has no lamp to disengage its secrets. We can be perfectly sure when we are in love even if the philosopher is dumb.

Now, we are perfectly ready to acknowledge this order and experience in such things as I have named. But a certain unwillingness arises when we turn to even greater matters of the spirit. When we direct our minds to the supreme spiritual realities we are inclined to argue that things are unreal unless the intellect can unravel their secrets and present them in luminous understanding. In these matters we talk and we reason as if reason were the only faculty of assurance. We argue as though intellect were everything. We speak as if we have no other power of apprehension. But we have many powers. We have powers of intuition. We have higher sense-perceptions which give us mystic sight, and taste, and touch. That was the Master's teaching to Nicodemus on this eventful night. He told him he could have assurance of spiritual reality long before he had powers of understanding.

The recognition and acceptance of this teaching would bring a great emancipation to many distressed and bewildered lives. They are giving undue ascendancy to the reason. Shall I say they are making life a monarchy, and they are placing reason on an unshared throne, when life is purposed to be a republic, with many powers in honourable office, and all sharing in holy sovereignty? There are intuitions, there are discernments, there are finer senses, spiritual instincts; there are powers affectional and spiritual as well as rational; and reality can impress itself upon these with such imperative compulsion that I am able to say: " I know that my Redeemer liveth." " I know Him in whom I believed." " The wind bloweth! " I know it! I hear it! I feel it! I may not be able to tell whence it cometh or whither it goeth, but I know it! Nothing can impair that final sense of real experience.

Now let us take the Master's teaching to some commanding mysteries which are nevertheless commanding realities. Take what we call the *mystery of reconciliation.* Is it a mystery? Yes. Is it also a reality? Yes. What is this reconciliation which is both reality and mystery? I wrote that question upon a paper before me on Tuesday morning. It was a gloomy and a heavy morning. Swift, massive, storm clouds were moving across the skies. Pelting rain and hail were falling. And then, in a moment, the clouds broke as if some powerful hand had torn a jet-black robe, and the sun shone through, and poured its warm and genial treasures upon me. And that, I think, is the scriptural figure of the spiritual happening when a man is reconciled to God. The clouds break, and the sun shines through! " Ye were once darkness, but now are ye light in the Lord." There is the darkness of guilt. Clouds of alienation roll between us and the Lord. And then the clouds are riven, and in the bright shining there is a glorious sense of at-oneness with the Light of life. We are conscious of rectified relationships. The soul is bathed in the friendly light of God's countenance. The ministry of forgiveness leads into the treasures of peace. "Lo, the winter is past, the rain is over and gone, the flowers appear on the earth, and the time of the singing of birds is come." Well, may I not know this reality of reconciliation? May I not be sure of it? May I not be as certain of it as Nicodemus was certain of the warm, wandering air of the spring-like April dawn? My soul is sure. I know!

But then intellect comes along, or reason, if you prefer the name, and she challenges the experience. "Now let us test it," she says. "Let us lay it all out in ordered analysis. Let us present it in the form of propositions. Let us see it in the form of a syllogism." Intellect says to me, "How can these things be?" I answer her challenge: "The wind bloweth, and I hear the sound thereof." "Yes," answers the intellect, "but whence doth the wind come, and whither does it go?" And I can only go a little part of the way in company with reason. I say to her, "God so loved the world that He gave His only begotten Son . . ." Reason impatiently answers, "Yes; but how, why, what, when?" And the questions of the intellect are not forbidden. She is not pursuing an unwarranted quest. She, too, is on the Father's business. But she soon puzzles me. She soon brings me to the frontiers of mystery where the darkness seems impenetrable.

My understanding falters and I have no key and no clue. But here is the blessed counsel of the Lord— reconciliation does not loiter until my intellect can explain. I can exult in the sunshine of God's countenance long before I can evolve a theory which will satisfy the intellectual schools. Some day reason will light her lamps along every road, and every place will be luminous with understanding.

Let us take the teachings of the Lord on the *mystery of the new creation.* This was the mystery which staggered the mind of Nicodemus, as he walked on the Mount of Olives with his Lord. There was reality and there was mystery; there was mystery, but there was reality. What is the statement of the mystery? We are told that life can shift its heredity. We are told that life can find another and a vital ancestry. The Master teaches that man can become related to a new Adam who is Christ the Lord. Let us state the mystery with the uttermost candour. The stream which flows from Adam's spring can be stopped, and a new stream can flow from a new fountain, and you and I can be found in the new succession. There are two lines of heredity, the Adam line and the Christ line, and a life can be transferred from one to the other. Life can find a new origin. It can have a new birth. It can flow in amazingly new issues. It can be born again in Christ.

That is a mystery? Yes, indeed. But then there is a mystery about the first birth. What do we

know about it? How much do we know about the
mystery of life? We know nothing! We know
nothing! What can reason tell me about that mysterious germ of life which followed some appointed
way of detachment, and formed itself into a separate whole and now is known as thee or me?
What does reason say about it? What has the
philosopher to say about life? I turn to one of
them and here is his answer: " Life is the principle
of animate corporal existence; the capacity of an
animal or plant for self-preservation and growth
by the processes of assimilation and excretion, the
permanent cessation of which constitutes death."
And so that is as far as intellect can take us in dis-
entangling the mystery of life! I call you to witness that the explanation is only a statement of the
mystery. It darkens counsel with words. It is a
lamp without light.

But the presence of the mystery need throw no
suspicion on the reality. The fact that intellect has
no light on life does not discredit our experience
of it. We know we *are,* even though we do not
know how we *became.* Life is an imperious presence even though intellect falters before her. " The
wind bloweth where it listeth and thou hearest the
sound thereof."

And as it is with the first birth, and with the
mystery and element of life, so it is with the second
birth and the mystery of the new creation. The intellect may not be able to ransack the treasury and

dispossess the secrets. But it is none the less real.
A man knows when his being is flooded with new
life. I knew in my home in Birmingham when our
water system had got communion with the Welsh
hills. The gathered treasures of those mist-
drenched heights flowed into my own house, and I
kne wit. And when we come into communion with
the Lord, who come that we might have life, and
that we might have it more abundantly, we know
it, we know it as a reality which cannot be questioned. We know it in richer fulness of being.
We know it in new avenues of relation. We know
it in new discernments. We know it in new delights. We know it in new griefs. We know it in
the new goals and the new roads to reach them.
We know it in new points of view and in new out-
looks. We know it in new correspondences with
God, and man, and the natural world. We know it
because we have a new heaven, and a new earth.
"The wind bloweth where it listeth!" There is
reality indeed. How can we doubt it? A man can
as soon doubt his creation in his mother's womb as
doubt his new creation in the renewing life of
Christ. The wind bloweth, he hears the sound
thereof! We are as sure of it as Nicodemus was
sure that he heard and felt those quickening airs of
the eastern dawn.

Mystery? Most certainly there is. And reason
comes along and challenges our experience. How
can these things be? How? How? How?

Trace the circle in intelligent understanding. I can only trace an infinitesmal part of a segment, the rest of the track is closed. How does God renew thy spirit by relating it to new springs? Thou canst not tell. How does God renew the perverted will? Thou canst not tell. How does God refresh the jaded emotions? Thou canst not tell. How does God recreate the prostituted affections? Thou canst not tell. How does God rekindle the smoking and smouldering conscience? How? How? How? And intellect cannot get the answers which make the circle luminous. And therefore intellect is inclined to say: "It is all delusion, pathetic and tragical." But she would not thus speak of the first life. Her inability to explain does not discredit the experience. Life precedes light. "One thing I know, that whereas I was blind, now I see." One thing I know, the wind is blowing! I hear it! I feel it! I am sure of it! But whence it cometh and whither it goeth I cannot tell. But I can wait. "Now I know in part, but then shall I know, even as also I am known." Meanwhile, "for me to live is Christ."

Let us take the counsels of the Master to another mystery, the *mystery of divine companionship*. And what is that? It is enshrined in the promise of the Master, "I am with you all the days." Here is a Friend who is always on the road. What kind of a road? Every sort of road. Through the green pastures and by the still waters! By the steep and rugged paths of righteousness! Through the valley of the shadow of death. Through landscapes crimson with the rose of Sharon! Through the trackless desert where the carrion eagle screams! Along the shining way to the marriage altar! Along the dripping way to the grave! The Friend is on every road.

And that Presence is to millions of people a wonderful reality. They have the impressive sense of a strong and chivalrous companion. "But warm, sweet, tender, even yet a present help is He." "The healing of His seamless dress is by our beds of pain." And there are some souls whose sense of communion with the Lord is so intimate that they feel that the removal of the thinnest veil would bring Him face to face. He brings them counsel when the roads are flinty. He bathes their bleeding feet. He imparts unto them strength for fine ventures. He gives them courage when the horizon is gloomy with the menace of the cross. "I will not leave thee nor forsake thee."

He is the great Friend on the road. Is it a reality? Yes, indeed. "Did not our hearts burn within us when He talked to us by the way?" Is it a mystery? Yes, indeed. And reason comes along questioning how these things can be. How? How? How? But reason stands abashed if she seeks to explain an earthly friendship. And the simpler the friendship the more difficult it is to give it intellectual analysis. And so with this supreme friendship of the Lord. My understanding cannot trace its means and its processes. Its treasures cannot be transferred to any intellectual laboratory. It passeth understanding. But the lameness of the intellect does not discredit the wholeness of the experience. The wind bloweth! I hear it! I feel it! I know it! "And His that gentle voice I hear, soft as the breath of even." "I know Him whom I have believed."

And so I appeal to you to honour the experimental faculties of your being as well as the faculty of reason. Give high place and office to your instincts, your intuitions, your affections, your faith, your hope. Follow the path of the noblest assumption. Fling yourself in the way of your faith, and follow it with the strength of a consecrated venture. Offer your life to the Saviour-hood and the governance of Christ. Do it as a sacred act of dedication, do it as a simple act of will. Let it be as an act in which you solemnly surrender your life to the highest. And you shall surely hear the wind that bloweth where it listeth.

XV

THE CHRIST OF TO-DAY

"Jesus Christ the same . . , to-day."—HEBREWS xiii. 8.

I WANT to notice just how this word emerges.
The road leading up to a text often yields the
secrets of its interpretation. Its momentum is
revealed in the prelude. We often miss the rich
significance of a word because we have not followed the track of the thought which leads up to it.
Over what sort of road, then, has the writer of this
great letter been travelling? He has been leading
his fellow-believers over a very wonderful road
which is trodden by pilgrims of faith. The road
is crowded with them. Everyone of the pilgrims
is radiant with victory. Everyone is distinguished
by some exploit. Everyone is carrying the palm of
a great venture. It is as if a procession were to
wind through the streets of our city, a procession
in which every man in the ranks breathes a spirit of
chivalry, and bears upon his breast the guerdons of
gallant conduct. Man after man strides along,
regiment after regiment, a perfect galaxy of courage and renown. And here is this nobler procession, the children of faith, marching along the way
of life, everyone wearing a cross of a more dis-

tinguished order, and all proclaiming their confidence in a Leader who never betrayed their trust. They have kindled their ardour at His fires. Their crusade was born in His will. Their triumphs were won in His grace. They rose out of frailty, for He gave them vigour. They shook off their timidities, for He gave them valour. In the power of His grace a menace is now an invitation, a difficulty is now a lure. They can do anything and everything in the equipment of His boundless resources. In Him they have strength, and exhilarancy, and buoyancy and song! Such is the radiant procession which winds up the pilgrim way, and as they march along I hear them sing: " Who shall dream of shrinking, by our Captain led? " These are the children of faith, and they are the men and women who do the impossible.

Such is the road over which the writer has been leading us. Now, when that road fades out of our eyes, and all its shining company with it, and we wake to reality as from a beautiful dream, when we find ourselves back on our own road—so drab, so heavy, so difficult, so unromantic—how then? That old procession, with its exploits and its songs —to look at it was like gazing upon a legendary world through the coloured lens of romance. But here is our road, the very real road which you and I have to travel to-day. It is a road ploughed into confusion by warfare. Old guide-posts have been broken down and have lost their use. Many old

lamps are blown out. Many comfortable, cosy
hostels are in ruin. A rugged and a troubled road
is ours, not much like a highway, but much more
like an uncertain and marshy track across a moor.
What, then, has this man to say to us, this man
who has been taking us over the romantic road of
faith? What has he to say to the men and women
of to-day? He has this to say, " Jesus Christ, the
same yesterday, to-day, and for ever!" Jesus
Christ, the same to-day! That is what he has to
say to us. The old Leader is on the new road.
There is no wasting of His resources. There is no
drought among the springs of grace. He is still
honouring faith by fellowship and power. He
acknowledges no mastery in hostile circumstances.
He pays no homage to hoary iniquities. He offers
the inexhaustible fountains of His own virtue and
strength. He answers faith with grace. He
crowns venture with triumph. He links the exploits of the fathers to the exploits of their children. The old Leader is on the new road, Jesus
Christ, the same yesterday, to-day and for ever.

" Jesus Christ, the same to-day!" Christ is not
an anachronism. The passing of the centuries does
not leave Him far behind. He is not a tale that is
told. He is as modern as our most modern necessities. He is as original as the most novel circumstance. He is level with our immediate task. He
keeps pace with the most startling and unexpected
challenge. Nay, the promise of the word is even

more than this; He not only keeps level with things, He goes before. He is always in front of the age. He is ever ahead with a more exacting call. As soon as we have grasped one achievement He is always in front striding out toward another. There is no final goal in this Leader's journeyings. He is ever ahead! " With the cross of Jesus going on before! " He is the same yesterday, and to-day and for ever.

" Jesus Christ to-day! " Is He ahead to-day? What is the challenge of to-day? And how does Christ Jesus meet it? Let us survey our circumstances. What do we see? *We see a great and contagious awakening of the democratic spirit.* The labouring man has been feeling out for his fellow-labourer, and in the grasp of his brother he has more than doubled his strength. The workman is emerging from his thraldom, and he is even now destroying the bulwarks of the feudalism in which he has so long been bound. He is asserting the dignity of his life, and he is proclaiming the royal prerogatives of manual toil. He is breaking up that heavy, unillumined, contemptuous word, " masses," and he is showing that behind the huddled term there are fine instincts, and large capacities, and noble passions. The Caliban of centuries is giving powerful witness that he has essential kinship with Ariel. Demos is emerging from contempt and he is laying his hands upon his inheritance, and claiming his sovereign rights. The democratic spirit is breathing over the face of the land, and it is the moving air of a new day.

Well, in all this, is Christ Jesus left far behind? Is He only the shining apparition of yesterday, and has He vanished with His age? Or is He a Leader for to-day, and can we proclaim Him to democracy as the Pioneer of all pioneers in the exploration of larger fellowships and nobler fraternity? Was He only the Christ of yesterday, or is He also the Christ of to-day? Has He anything for democracy, or must democracy seek its treasure elsewhere? Let us look at Him. When He came among us to reveal the life and character of God, He housed His holy body in the narrow circle of a working-man. In His boyhood He donned the workman's apron, and for thirty years, in a little market town, He served His fellows as the village carpenter. He was the bread-winner for a widowed mother, the eldest son of a large family. He knew the workman's lot, and if He be now alive how can labour be to Him anything but something noble and venerable, and how can He regard the apron of the worker as anything but one of the robes of righteousness and one of the garments of salvation?

When He emerged from the workshop to establish His Kingdom He sought the nucleus of the fellowship among the working men. He chose twelve men, and He found the majority of them among the working class. He knew the stuff He

chose. It was very awkward and difficult stuff.
He sought to shape it, but it easily lost the shape in
which He tried to fashion it. It was almost like
giving a shape to water. But He knew the worth
of the men, and He held on to them with indomit-
able patience. And in the long run He made out
of these plastic workmen brave knights who could
dare to challenge kings, and who could march as to
a wedding to face the menace of death. "Having
loved His own He loved them unto the end." And
if Christ Jesus is still alive, if He is the same to-
day, does anyone doubt that He befriends the common toiler, and that He goes before him to prepare
his ways?

But now watch this great Democrat. Examine
His teachings. All His basal principles breathe the
democratic spirit. His teaching spurns the established boundaries. It leaps across conventional
gulfs, across the deep chasms which yawn between
race and race, between class and mass, between sex
and sex, and between sect and sect. Dip into His
teachings where you please, and follow the breadth
of its democratic inclusiveness. Take any commandment; who is outside the range of its decree?
Or take any beatitude and trace the range of its
orbit; who is omitted from the circle of its bounty?
Or take any of the larger teachings which blaze like
planets in the moral and spiritual firmament. Here
is a little cluster of them and I would have you
mark the amplitude of their range—all races and

peoples are of equal sacredness; character is more important than talent; responsibility is measured according to endowment; neighbourliness is to be defined by the circle of necessity and not by the limitations of race; the success of life is to be measured by its secret fidelities and not by its popular triumphs. That is only a little handful of the principles of Jesus, and they are typical of all the rest, and I ask you what you think of their depth and comprehension, and how you regard the vigour of their democratic spirit. What labour leader to-day, what pioneer is in front of this Jesus in the vital proclamation of democratic worth?

And if you would have the consummation of democratic expression let me ask you to take this pregnant word of our Lord: " One is your Master, and all ye are brethren." Who is ahead of that great word in spirit, and in vision, and in quest? Christ is the first and the greatest of all democrats, and if ours is the age when democracy is awaking, Christ is its anointed Leader and Pioneer. Christ thinks in terms of the world, and He would make men citizens of the universe. He answers this challenge of the age, for Christ Jesus is the same yesterday, to-day, and for ever. He is always going on before.

I will listen to another challenge which is to-day sounded loudly down every street of our national life: *I mean the challenge of men who are seeking a richer material inheritance.* We cannot turn our eyes without seeing the challenge, we cannot open our ears without hearing it. Men and women are everywhere reaching out for more of the life and comfort which can be found in material things. Do you wonder at it? We may perhaps have been irritated by the miners, and perhaps we have been repelled by their somewhat blind and selfish aggression. Have you ever spent even a couple of hours in the gloomy, clammy hole where the miner earns his daily bread? Have you seen him emerging from the mine, and especially have you seen him in old age with bowed body, bent out of natural shape and posture? Have you been into the miner's house, which he has to call his home, a place which is often little better than the gloomy place where he earns his bread? I do not wonder that his hands are stretched out for more human comforts and for a larger share in the fulness of God's bountiful world. And it is even so with the factory operative. They are seeking an escape from the dull, grey monotony of daily circumstance. They are seeking more of the world's treasure, more of its leisure, more of its pleasure. They want the iron gate to be opened which imprisons their youth. They want the heaviness to be lightened which burdens their prime. They want the menace to be taken out of old age, they want their years to glide into,

> An old age serene and bright,
> And lovely as a Lapland night.

Well, in all these challenging demands how fares it with the Christ? Is He away back in other days? Is He out of touch with grim necessity? Is His teaching an exhausted specific? Have all His goals been reached and left behind? Go into His life and look at Him. What is He doing? He is seeking life and joy for everybody, life and joy in widest commonality spread. On every side He is opening out life's possibilities, unveiling capacities which He wants all men to possess and exercise. You cannot think of this Christ as being satisfied with any conditions which cramps life, and which sterilizes growth, and creates a dwarf. It is altogether incongruous to imagine Christ contented that a man's life should be like a caged bird, or like some bleached and anæmic plant in a sunless cellar. " I am come that ye might have life, and that ye might have it more abundantly." I know that the word is elemental, fundamental, and fontal. I know that this was the purpose of His coming, but I for one will draw no petty boundaries within which His treasure is confined. The aim of Christ is a man made whole, liberated to his full capacity in body, mind and soul. " He shall be like a tree planted by rivers of water." That is the figure which His own inspired word offers to us as a fitting symbol—a healthy tree—a tree, rooted in ample resources, and reaching out on every side in symmetrical strength and beauty. Try to feel the energy of the figure, appreciate the grace of it,

realize its every-sided loveliness, and then think of
a miner, or of a fireman on a liner, or any typical
workman at one of a hundred posts, and then tell
me how far he is away from his inheritance purposed by his Lord. Let us fix the contrast in mind,
the contrast between a nobly proportioned tree and
a man denied his full development.

> Then Christ sought out an artisan,
> A low-browed, stunted, haggard man,
> And a motherless girl, whose fingers thin
> Pushed from her faintly want and sin.
>
> These set He in the midst of them,
> And as they drew back their garment-hem
> For fear of defilement, " Lo, here," said He,
> The " images ye have made of Me! "

Aye, but in His aim, and in His own spirit and
reach, Christ is more than on a level with modern
aspiration. If a workman says, " I am reaching
out," Christ reaches with him, and beyond the
man's reach, and He would pass through every
darkening barrier into larger life and freedom.
Verily, He is not only the Christ of yesterday, He
is the Christ of to-day; Jesus Christ, the same yesterday, to-day, and for ever.

But I cannot stop here when I am reviewing the
competency of the Saviour to meet the demands of
to-day. We have been listening to the challenging
cries of necessities which are ringing down our
public streets. But there are necessities which do

not march with banners, nor do they cry aloud at the corners of the streets, and they are all the more profound because they move in secret. Better wages do not hold the clue to final freedom. Money itself is not the pledge of vital growth. A finer house may not make a nobler home. A bit of beautiful garden may not clothe its holder with moral strength and beauty. A man may add acres to his material inheritance and yet add nothing to his moral and spiritual stature. He may increase in goods while he himself is an arrested growth. There are necessities of deeper import than any I have named, and if these are ignored or unreached a man can never find his destined freedom. You may enrich a man as you please with material advantage, but after all the man is in bonds.

How, then, is it with Christ and this imperious necessity? Is He up-to-date? Is He level with this exacting demand? Or does it leave Him far behind? Nay, He can deal with it. Deal with what? He can deal with sin, sin which lurks in the heart of a workman, and sin that hides in the heart of a peer. Sin? That is not a modern term. No, but it is a modern thing. I grant that if you search the labour papers through and through, or if you search the organs of the aristocracy, you will never find the word sin. It is not allowed to show its face in print. It seems a troublesome word. Or it seems to be an obsolete word, about as insignificant as the word selah, and it is given no place in the busy vital currency of our modern terminology. Indeed, some of these papers tell us that the word is just a poor remnant of an old theological invention, and it is now justly relegated to a sort of museum, where rest the discarded remains of myth and legend. The thing itself is an unreal ghost which priests have conjured up, and it is being kept alive in priestly interests to disturb the souls of men.

But when any man, miner or peer, goes quietly and alone to the deep waters of his own soul, and gazes into their depths, he sees something which is very real and which is the enemy of his peace. The term sin may mystify him, but he knows the thing it represents. He knows when an act of usurpation is committed in the soul. He knows when an unclean passion steals out of its lair and crosses the boundary line, and takes the throne. He knows what he ought to do with it. " Thou shalt tread upon the lion and the adder, the young lion and the dragon shalt thou trample under feet." He knows when his inner life is dislocated. He knows when a crooked thing wriggles through his soul. He knows when the flag of rebellion is uplifted in the secret place. He knows when he defies God. Get a man quietly to himself, and whether he be a man with a pound a week, or a man with a hundred pounds a week, if his eyes be turned to the deeper things he will confess that there is sin in him, and there is guilt, and that these two have a momentum which holds his life in degrading course and currency.

Well, what about Jesus the Christ? When He faces this necessity is He up-to-date? Can He deal with it? Can He "cleanse the stuffed bosom of that perilous stuff which weighs upon the heart?" Yes, indeed He can. Can He cleanse the springs of passion? Yes, indeed He can. Can He change the climate of a temperament? Can He take a vagrant soul and bring it to its home in God? Yes, indeed He can. Can He purify and beautify a wasted spirit and set it on its throne? Yes, indeed He can. Jesus can give a man freedom where alone freedom has her royal seat. Christ's freedom is freedom which means spiritual power. It is freedom which means moral force. Christ creates within a man a secret wealth of vitality which is like a well of water springing up into everlasting life, and in the amplitude of His moral resources all things become possible unto Him.

If Christ can do these wonderful things, and He can, and if we believe it, as we do, let us tell the world about it, let us speak with the same confidence, and with the same impatient eagerness which a man would use were he making known that he had found a perfect cure for cancer. I want a witness that will cut right through loitering ambiguities as a breeze from the mountains would disturb the stagnant air in a fusty room. I present the Christ to you as the Christ of to-day. He is the greatest of all democrats, far ahead of the boldest of all. He is the Pioneer in all human enlargement, with a programme bigger than all. And He is the incomparable Emancipator, descending into depths of secret bondage where no-one else can follow. I present Him to you, the Christ, as the Saviour of to-day—Christ Jesus, the same yesterday, to-day, and for ever.

> All hail the power of Jesus' name,
>   Let angels prostrate fall,
> Bring forth the royal diadem,
>   And crown Him Lord of all.

Printed in United States of America.